TEACHERS' VOICES, TEACHERS' WISDOM

SEVEN
ADVENTUROUS
TEACHERS
THINK
ALOUD

•

NANCY KREINBERG & HARRIET NATHAN

EQUALS
Lawrence Hall of Science
University of California at Berkeley
1991

The Lawrence Hall of Science is a public science center, teacher inservice institution, and research unit in science education at the University of California at Berkeley. For many years, it has developed curricula and teaching strategies to improve mathematics and science education at all levels, and to increase public understanding of, and interest in, science and mathematics.

Design: Tim Erickson

Cover Design: Carol Bevilacqua

Photographs: Richard Hoyt

Library of Congress Cataloging-in-Publication Data

Teachers' voices, teachers' wisdom: seven adventurous teachers think aloud /
    Nancy Kreinberg and Harriet Nathan, [editors].
            p.   cm.
        Includes bibliographical references and index.
        ISBN 0-912511-55-9
        1. Teachers—California—San Francisco Bay Area—Interviews.
    2. Public Schools—California—San Francisco Bay Area. 3. Teaching.
    I. Kreinberg, Nancy. II. Nathan, Harriet.
    LB1775.3.C2T43   1991
    371.1'0092'2—dc20

                                        91-25315
                                        CIP

The views expressed herein are those of the narrators or the writers and do not reflect those of the University of California, the Lawrence Hall of Science, or the Carnegie Corporation of New York.

Printed in the United States of America
Printing (last digit): 9 8 7 6 5 4 3 2 1

To the seven teachers
whose voices and wisdom inspired and formed this book:

Grace Coates

Frank Gold

Elois Irvin

Nan Jackson

Suzy Ronfeldt

Sallyann Tomlin

Bob Whitlow

CONTENTS

FOREWORD

This is an invitation to listen to seven inspired teachers as they think aloud about their students and themselves, their preparation for teaching, their early years as teachers, their insights and beliefs. Next, we invite you to examine your own assumptions and ideas about public education today. Whether you are a teacher, parent, administrator, policy maker, or other concerned citizen, these gifted teachers speak directly to you.

We met these teachers through EQUALS. They are among the 5,000 teachers in California who sought out this program, which focuses on mathematics equity and challenges traditional assumptions about who can do mathematics. (EQUALS is described more fully in the Introduction that follows.)

The interviews are individual, tape-recorded conversations conducted in the San Francisco Bay Area in 1987 and 1988, transcribed, and submitted to the teacher/narrators who reviewed them for accuracy. For ease of reading, and with the concurrence of the narrators, the interview questions have been implied or incorporated in the narrations. The writers have rearranged some sequences, but have not changed the teachers' words, which provide a self-portrait of each teacher at a specific time. The teachers are not part of a survey nor representatives of any group, yet the realities they express reflect the conflicts and the hopes that many teachers experience.

The teachers' words are not interrupted by editorial insertions or interpretations. Instead, subheads serve as guideposts for following the teachers' discussions in sequence, or browsing among a variety of ideas and concerns.

The teachers responded to the interview process with thoughtfulness, wit, and candor. Similarly, we now ask much of the reader: to be a thoughtful listener, a critical thinker, and one who chooses to act on behalf of public education. What some of the teachers say may accord with your views, other portions may not, but their conversations are intended to stimulate your own thinking and move you toward positive action.

The teachers' voices are the heart of the book. Each part explores the ways teachers experience and work in a series of ever-widening relationships and responsibilities—personal, professional, and political: Part 1, Becoming a Good Teacher; Part 2, Inside the Classroom and the Profession; Part 3, A Place for Adventurers; and Part 4, The Politics of Education. The writers' interpretations and proposals, presented in the Afterword, draw on many of the teachers' ideas, as well as research from other sources and our own understanding and experience.

We are grateful for the creativity and support of the EQUALS staff who, along with the seven teachers, represent what is best in education. Special thanks are due to Linda Witnov for her expert transcription and to Tim Erickson for his creativity in designing the book.

We very much appreciate the help of the following people in reviewing the manuscript and providing valuable insights that helped to develop our thinking and refine our ideas: Kathleen Devaney, Carol Newman, Judith Warren Little, Judith Quinn, Eleanor Linn, Ann Nathan-Johnson, Elinor Bernal, Edward Nathan, Kay Gilliland, Marc Levin, Terry Dean, and Ron Heckart.

We are fortunate to be based at the Lawrence Hall of Science, a lively and rewarding intellectual home. Director Marian Diamond, and the many staff members of the Hall, are dedicated to adults' and children's learning.

We gratefully acknowledge the encouragement and support of the Carnegie Corporation of New York and especially appreciate their long-term commitment to the teaching profession.

Nancy Kreinberg and Harriet Nathan
Berkeley 1991

INTRODUCTION

Come with us into the classroom and bring a child you know and care about. Is this child eager, expecting to find excitement and success, or reluctant, fearing trouble and failure? Think about the kinds of experiences this child should have, each day, in school. Think about the kind of teacher you want for this child.

The relationship between student and teacher is the core of what happens in the classroom. One hopes for a teacher able to respect individual children and their contributions, and to provide ways for each child to be successful. You are about to discover seven teachers who do this.

As teachers in elementary or high schools, they are secure, willing to take risks, and creative enough to find new opportunities for professional growth. They all shared the experience of taking part in EQUALS, a program initiated in 1977 at the Lawrence Hall of Science, University of California at Berkeley.

The EQUALS program helps K–12 teachers retain more females and students of color in mathematics, responding to the fact that students filtered out of mathematics courses are predominantly poor, of color, and/or female. Teachers who participate in the 30-hour EQUALS workshops conduct research studies in their classrooms, engage in problem solving activities and discussions, explore topics such as alternative assessment and cooperative learning, and, most importantly, share with other teachers methods that have been effective for them. The workshops also provide role models to stimulate interest in math and science careers and cultivate leadership skills to help teachers spread the EQUALS methods and materials to interested colleagues.

Nationwide, more than 53,000 teachers in 36 states have participated in EQUALS. The program now includes EQUALS centers in 10 states and several foreign countries, a publication series, and the innovative FAMILY MATH program, which enables parents and children to enjoy and learn mathematics together.

In selecting teachers to interview, we found a true embarrassment of riches because so many in EQUALS were outstanding. We recognized these seven as exemplars of the best in American education. They came from a range of communities, backgrounds, grade levels, and teaching experiences.

The conditions of teaching circumscribe what even the best teachers can do. The public has a tendency to search everywhere for inspiration and solutions to problems of public education, rather than altering conditions under which teachers work. A prevalent belief holds that the teachers' personality traits account for the bulk of what they are able to accomplish in the classroom; and that if we could just find and hire enough of the right people, problems of educational quality and the roadblocks to learning would go away. Unfortunately, as these teachers tell us, the facts do not support this easy solution.

Our public education system is failing many children, especially those who are poor and of color. The voices of these teachers signal a way out of the current and ongoing crises in education. By listening to what they say, and having the courage to do what they ask, we have an opportunity to change a stalled system that works only moderately well for many students, and not at all for some.

The classroom doors of four elementary schools and three high schools are opening, and you will meet seven extraordinary people, all of them teachers.

Part 1

BECOMING A GOOD TEACHER

Most of us have been to school. Experiences differ, but we can still remember a favorite teacher who helped, and sometimes one who did not. As children, we could recognize the good ones who opened doors of interest, opportunity, and high expectations, sometimes inviting and sometimes shoving us through. Occasionally, now, when we meet people who are teachers, we wonder how they would compare with those in our memories, but the teaching profession is not one that stimulates curiosity outside the profession. We think we know enough about teaching and teachers. But do we?

When we take a closer look at teachers and public education, some underlying questions arise. Where do good teachers come from? What brings people to teaching and what keeps good teachers in the profession? How does a promising teacher evolve into a good one? How does a good teacher become excellent?

Grace Coates' story provides some answers. For her, teaching remains an unending source of curiosity and challenge. She sees extraordinary possibilities in what she and her students can learn and accomplish.

Grace Coates

Grace Coates: Professionalism, Pride, and Diversity

My Life in Grade School

My whole school experience was negative. That sounds awful for me to say, but…(laughs). I didn't speak English until about 3rd or 4th grade, and at that it was broken, choppy English. My parents were from Mexico and my older brothers and sisters spoke Spanish at home with my parents. Because they came here as older kids, it was a little more difficult for them to acquire the language.

I went through one school in Union City [California], from kindergarten through 6th grade. I remember having various teachers who were not necessarily negative influences and not necessarily great, positive experiences. Nobody really stands out. The principal there was always very involved with my family; it was a family of 12. There were financial problems and he used to kind of help—making sure my mom and dad had access to things they needed. He would refer us to places where they could get clothes and that sort of thing.

The nurse was always calling us in. You have to realize that in a family of 12 there is always one thing or another with somebody. But I think the most typical problem was that one or two of us always had lice. It was just that kind of community. So now when my kids at school have lice I say, "It's no big deal. You do this and you do that and it's gone." But I remember.

When I Could Speak Spanish in School

We were not allowed to speak Spanish in school, but I remember being allowed to speak Spanish in school and not feeling bad about it during 5th and 6th grade. The principal called us into the office to translate to the secretary for the newcomers when they came to register their kids.

When I was in 4th grade I had a teacher named Mr. Monteverde. Now, you don't get much more Spanish than that, you can almost hear the lisp. He was short and brown and Indian-looking like my dad. He was very stern, and I'm positive that he spoke Spanish, but he never did to us.

There were many Spanish-speaking kids in the school. It was a Mexican community. Union City used to have 10,000 people living there, and most of them were the Mexican community that worked in the surrounding fields. It was a migrant community, but there was no bilingual program.

The whole community was poor, so we were like everybody else, only we were poorer because there were more of us. Everybody there was kind of in the same boat, so comparatively, I never felt poor or different until I was in junior high or high school. When we moved to Hayward, then I saw that other people lived in different neighborhoods and I saw that the differences were great. As I look back, I didn't feel weird or ostracized.

Seeing President Kennedy and Hearing Robert Frost

Out of all my K–6 experiences in school, the only thing I remember was that I got to see President Kennedy. I might have been in 6th grade; President Kennedy came to UC Berkeley with Robert Frost and they had this big to-do at the stadium. We were all required to take some sort of test to choose which ones of us would get to go to this thing. It was a like a field trip for a limited few.

I took the test and passed it, and my father said, "Well, she's not going," because I was never allowed to go on field trips. The women in my family went to school and we came home and we stayed home, so for him it was an unnecessary thing to do. Then I remember a teacher coming to speak to my father, to tell him what a significant opportunity it was for me to go. It was memorable. It was the first place I'd ever been where there were that many people, where there was a poet.

My big escape through school was that I read a lot. Initially, I read whatever I could get hold of in Spanish—all my mother's adult romances, for example. Later on, in 4th, 5th, and 6th grade, I started reading poetry and real literature. It was my form of escape, just to go away and be quiet. I was really impressed by that because I had read Robert Frost and I was going to get to go hear him. That meant more to me, at that time, than seeing President Kennedy.

Two Phone Calls

The way I became a teacher is bizarre. I graduated from high school in June and was married in January. I was unemployed for a while. As a teenager I used to work in a rest home when the attendant went out in the evening, so I had experience in that. About my 23rd birthday I decided to go out and get a job and I did two things: one, I applied at a rest home because they needed a cook, and I went through an employment service. I thought, "Well, I can do that, I've cooked all my life, with my mom for all these kids." Second, I took a test—it really intimidated me to take a test—with the school district, for a position as a Spanish bilingual instructional aide. I did those two things within a day or two of each other and then I waited to hear.

It just so happened that the Hayward School District called me first the same day that the rest home lady called to say, "We need you to come to cook tonight." I said, "Oh, no, I have an appointment, an interview." So I went to Hayward and I was interviewed by three or four people, a principal, and some teachers, and I got hired that same day.* The fact that I ended up in the classroom was a matter of who called me back first. I became an instructional aide in a bilingual class and did that for about seven or eight years.

Learning to Teach

When I went to college to take instructional aide classes, they were terribly disappointing. The classes were boring to me because they were how to run the film projector and how to put up bulletin boards. They were all the "how to do" physical labor parts of being a teacher and none of the "how to help the child" kind of stuff. So that really bothered me and I dropped out of it.

The teacher in my second job—oh, gosh, she was a wonderful, wonderful individual. She was the kind of person who was always cheerful and happy and loving, and the kids really loved her. Academically she was very traditional in her teaching. She had a set way of doing things.

---

*In September 1990, the Hayward Unified School District enrolled 19,143 students and employed 1,265 teachers in 23 elementary schools, 5 intermediate schools, and 4 comprehensive high schools. The student population was 13.5% African American; 6.9% Asian; 6.9% Filipino/Pacific Islander; 29.8% Hispanic; .6% Native American; and 42.1% White. Twenty-one percent of the families of students in the Hayward District received Aid to Families with Dependent Children (AFDC) in Fall 1990.

I guess what I learned from Lisa was simply how to deal with kids all the time and how to deal with their parents. She was always a positive person, her personality was always up. In terms of real teaching, what I learned was basically what I did with the children, because they were given to me. She gave me a lot of freedom to work with the kids. I don't think Lisa said, "I'm going to give you all this freedom," it was that "We have all these kids and we all have to do something."

Helping Women Help Their Kids

I really enjoyed working as an instructional aide, because to me it was like getting to go back to school under different circumstances. Also there were a lot of Mexican parents at the school who needed constant assistance, so we were always dealing with them.

I worked with a teacher who was not bilingual but had learned Spanish in school. I even had to go and tell the person who did the bilingual program that she spoke enough Spanish to function in the classroom, but she didn't have a sense of the nuances and the cultural things that come with the language. I figured that, if she spoke enough to teach colors and numbers and that sort of thing, I could pick up the rest, which is kind of the way it worked. Her attitude and my attitude were really different for the families that came to us for various kinds of help.

My attitude was that you want to help them help themselves; her attitude was that you want to help them. I always felt that she was trying to do for them, take them here, get them that, do this. I was always saying, "Well, if two of the adult ladies come with me to get the kids their shots, then I'll take them to get their shots. Then I'll say, 'If two of you do this, I'll show you where the bus stop is to get to the welfare department.'" But this teacher was more into, "Well, can't you just take them? Can't you just do it?"

I always felt, "What do you do when we're gone?" and to this day I function on that level. "You need to do these things when I'm gone." So, I always encouraged the women that I dealt with in these families to get out, and look, and take charge.

Who Teaches the Sweat Hogs?

While I was still an aide, I moved into doing more instruction because of the double language that goes on in the classroom. Somebody has to take either a group of kids learning Spanish or a group of kids learning English. When I was an instructional aide, I usually took a group learning English, to listen to them read or do their seat work with them.

It was about two years into that, that I actually just started doing the lessons, taking the teacher's manual, looking at it, seeing what had to be done, where they were, and where they were going. I did what was called "20-20-20": the teacher had them for 20 minutes, I had them for 20 minutes, and they had seat work for 20 minutes, so there was a lot more real teaching that went on. Usually I got the really low-achieving kids, and they knew it, they knew who they were. As one kid said, "Why do you always get the sweat hogs?" I said, "You guys aren't the sweat hogs." He said "Yes we are." They knew.

It was always my vision then that I shouldn't have these kids, that as an aide I should have the high-achieving kids and the teacher should have these kids. I do this now in my classroom: I take all the kids who need the extra help, who need me, and my instructional aide takes the kids who are functioning really well. But when I was an aide it was done the opposite way, and it still is in many classrooms. The instructional aide will get the children who need all the extra help, but who's trained to provide that?

A Foot on the Career Ladder

There was federal money under Title VII to send instructional aides to school as a career ladder program. They interviewed about seven or eight people, and then they sent us to Cal State Hayward. They paid our tuition and our books and gave us a set amount of money. We all started as a group. There were people within the Title VII Project that were really supportive, and they basically said, "If you commit yourself to go to this, we'll commit ourselves to help you." I was working as an instructional aide during the day and going to school in the afternoons or the evenings. At this point both of my boys were in school and my sisters would help me with the kids.

The first thing that I took was public speaking, because I would be the last person to ever get up in front of a group and say anything. Everybody at Cal State Hayward said that the only thing that's required is that you must take public speaking first, and so I took it. It was at that point that I really got into talking and expressing myself and not backing down. Before that I used to say, "Well, OK, maybe they know more or maybe they're smarter, or maybe...something." I decided after that to take another public speaking class through adult school, for my own personal good.

In my credential year, my math teacher taught us the way you should teach math to kids, using objects to teach with; letting us explore with all the materials. I said, "Why is he having us do this?" and people would sit there and say, "I don't need to be playing with this stuff." But that wasn't the point. He wanted us to go through a process. He didn't tell us that; he just said, "We're going to do this," and then he had us put a presentation together.

It didn't really match what I did in the classroom, but it matched what I later would think up doing in my own classroom. It was hard for me to articulate why we did it and if somebody asked why, I probably couldn't at that time have said why—just that we did, and it helped the kids. Now I could say why.

The First to Graduate

You have to consider that in high school my two older sisters and my brother had dropped out before me. I was the first kid in my family to graduate, and then the only kid after that until the last daughter would graduate. My parents used to look at it this way; they would give us a watch at 8th grade. If you've made it through 8th grade, you've done really well.

The college courses were hard for me because I had not been prepared for them in high school. In high school I took whatever math you take when you were not going to college: I took business math, checkbook math, I took pre-algebra and did really poorly. I don't think I would have done any better if I had had a better teacher, either.

My natural insight and sense of putting things together and making connections I think is what helped me through those classes. I knew all along that I was heading for the credential program. Oh, I went crazy. When I went into the credential program, it was like I could see the light at the end of the tunnel, and I just ran for it. I remember taking an ungodly load. That first fall in my credential program I think I took 24 units and worked full time. I mean, it was nuts. When I look back, I wonder, "How did I do that?"

Looking Like a Teacher

The first day I came onto this campus as a bilingual teacher after Marcos hired me, I was walking down the hall with a box of goodies to room 9, my classroom. There were two teachers standing in the hallway and I said, "Excuse me. Could you tell me where room 9 is?" and one said, "Well, who are you?" I said, "I'm Grace Coates and I'm going to be teaching in room 9." She said, "Well, that's funny, you don't look like a teacher."

I looked at them and I thought, "That's really peculiar." I didn't know why I didn't look like a teacher, but whatever it was, I was glad that I didn't, because I always thought teachers were kind of up-tight looking or repressed. It didn't dawn on me until later that they had really meant to insult me. It is OK in retrospect, because now all three of us are good friends. I even told one of them that I remember her first comment to me and she laughed.

Sticking by the Book Until the Light Goes On

When I began teaching, everything was very structured for me. Basically it was safe for me as a new teacher to stick by the book and go sequentially—to take the math book and try to get at least to the beginning of multiplication by May, and schedule the work in such a manner that this would happen. I also used to be very test-oriented because I really did want my kids to know certain things by the time the test came. The biggest change in me is not being bound to structures, and having the feeling to trust myself when I create something and say, "This is a go because you know it."

The best way I can say it is, "when the light goes on." I was writing their homework at my computer one day, and a certain sequence was coming up over and over. I realized that I did have a sense of all the different levels of cognition, and a sense of all the reasons why these things were in my homework. Before, I might have stuck them in because I read them in a book, or because so-and-so did it this way, or it really went well with Bloom's Taxonomy,[1] or because of something that I had been taught. This was, "Holy cow, I've really internalized all this stuff."

It may change down the road, that's OK, but the fact was that I was sitting there writing, and didn't need to ask, "Tell me what else I could do?" I felt good realizing that. I think that's the biggest change. I feel that if you gave me an empty classroom, with *nada*, that I could go in and teach everything that needed to be taught, at least for K, 1, 2, and 3. I wouldn't need a book; I might even prefer not to have a book. That's how I'm teaching now. The work sheets go home for homework and the good stuff happens in the classroom.

Complex Instruction Program

An important event for me was participating in the Complex Instruction program at Stanford.[2] This is a program that assists teachers in establishing heterogeneous classroom groups, where the teacher and students have to live by and adhere to certain norms. Everybody has a job, and that job is to be taken seriously and is to be given value because in real life all those jobs relate to something that you do outside the classroom.

The teacher's job is not to disempower kids by doing things for them, but to ask questions that extend their thinking, as well as substantive questions. There are questions that can be answered factually, as well as questions that take you off on a tangent. The teacher needs to be able to make connections with what the students are doing now, how it relates to the real world, how it relates to adults we know, how it relates to jobs of status, or jobs of no status. It doesn't really matter, just that the teacher connects it.

The teacher has to be able to give specific feedback to students, to give them a sense of intellectual value and contribution within the group. So although everything is happening in a group, there is space for the individual to shine. The way we were taught to do it is to pick children who were low-status— and I hate that word but that's the word they gave us—children who were either low-status academically, socially, or in the way their peers looked at them, in any way that was other than equal.

If I took a popularity vote in my class everybody would tell you who was the smartest, who was the most artistic. Kids are always assigned a role by their peers, and so the teacher's job in this situation is to give everybody a sense of worth—a sense of real worth, not just a warm fuzzy. You know the difference? It really bugs me, that's another thing with me, "self-esteem" classes...(laughs), well, that's a whole other tangent.

The teacher does this work with the kids and it is hoped that what happens by the end of the year is that everybody in that classroom has a sense of the value of each individual. You're supposed to target a few and elevate their status, but if you've done it right, you've done it for everybody. I have seen it in my classroom every year.

I have seen my frustration at the beginning of the year when these kids don't work well together, when they fight, when they bicker, when they don't show consideration, and the way I feel at the end of the year when kids are saying things to each other like, "Could you please help me with this building because you know how to make really good buildings?" Or "Could you please draw this for me?" and then the other kid will say, "Oh, no, I won't do it for you, but here's how you can do it." It's not fake and it's not something that you just said because teacher said, "Now everybody tell each other one nice thing." It's not like that at all. To me that's empty. I don't think kids get into that; they know it's empty too.

I think that kids are really perceptive of what is the truth and what is real. If I were feeding kids a line of bull, if I were saying to kids, "You really should be this and you really should be that," if I were full of "shoulds" and "oughts," kids would really turn off to me. If I say to them, "You know, if you do this, this will happen and that will happen. What do you think?" the kids will say, "Yeah, yeah, maybe." They're still skeptical, but "yeah, maybe," and that opens the door and lets them in.

Looking for Something Good

Implementing the Complex Instruction program rests partly on the teacher, what she or he can see to bring out. When I did the training, the hardest part for me was to go up to a group and say, "Oh, I see you're a really accurate measurer and that's helpful when you become a mechanic or something..." You just can't do that. What you have to say is, "You measure really accurately. Doctors have to be good at that." Walk away from it. What has this kid done? He measured accurately. Doctors do that, wow.

Later on in the wrap-up I say, "Why do doctors have to measure accurately? Who cares? Well, what if your doctor asked your mom to give you two or three of these pills every hour instead of one-and-a-half every four hours? Think about it." Then the kids start making connections. Who else needs to measure accurately? They think how it's such a minor thing, measuring accurately, and it's connected in the most profound ways.

I really love art, being able to envision something. If I say to a kid, "How did you get this picture?" "Oh, it's in my head." They think it's nothing. I say, "You saw this in your head before it was on the paper? My God, great artists do that," and I walk away. I'll say, "I cannot do that. You guys give me a paint-by-numbers picture, I'm really good at that. I can follow instructions, but I can't make a picture." Then we talk about it. It leads into judging art, having taste for art, what is good art, what is bad art?

This is 2nd grade, it can happen, and you don't have to give up a lot of time for it, either. It just leads to wonderful things: kids as artists, kids in 2nd grade with no training, but they understand perspective. I talk about how I never learned about perspective until high school, and ask, "How come you know it now?" Well, this kid's all of a sudden in high school in his brain. So it's just a little tiny shot that you give them, and you walk off.

How do kids learn to give self-esteem to each other? I might say, "Today I want you guys to look at your group and notice just one thing about each person, what he or she is doing that's good." Well, obviously, if you know that each person is looking at you to see if you're doing something good, you're going to do something good because somebody is looking for it. The reporter is going to report.

Now, when he gets up to report, I'm not going to ask him to report on everybody and what they all did that was good. I'm going to say, "Tell me one person who did one thing that helped your group," and then he talks about one person. So even though he only spoke of one person he thought about five people, and that's the ripple effect: a whole bunch of people got it but only one was spoken of. Tomorrow he might look for something else. But you want to keep it short because kids get really bored with it fast and then it's not sincere, it's not real.

The Seeds of Self-Esteem

I say to my kids, "If I'm sitting at my desk doing my make-up, am I being a good teacher?" I make them evaluate me, and I make them see me for the job I owe them, and I tell them that. "When you leave this class, you're going to have lots of different teachers. You're going to have teachers for the next x years."

"There's something you must remember, that they are there for you. You're not there for them. They are there for you. So, what are you going to do to make sure that they do the best for you? What's your part?" Kids hook into that, too. Now, maybe these kids will drop out, maybe some will get pregnant, you never know what's going to happen, but you do know that you put a seed there.

If I ask my kids, "Who gave you this A?" "Myself." "Who gave you this F?" "Myself." I don't think that I put the esteem in them. I think that I need to know how to let them put it in themselves. Because what's up when I'm gone? Who's going to put it there then?

Fascinated by Kids

My relationship with kids is the one thing that's remained constant. Kids have always been nuts about me, and I'm not sure that I've always been nuts about them. Mind you, I come from a family of 12. When I got married, I wanted no children, but my husband wanted four, so we had two. It was a big tease that it was my compromise.

I've never really felt like, "Kids are the greatest thing in the world." I look at them more in awe, with a profound sense of "Here's this human being." I'm always fascinated by kids, how some kids just buckle under and how some kids' spirits soar above all the problems that they go through. But kids usually like me and, if there is a kid who doesn't like me, the rest of the class is in shock. "So and so doesn't like you."

They'll all run and tell me. They'll squeal on this poor individual and so then I have to talk about how you have to go through life and you cannot possibly like everyone you meet, and that there's sometimes a reason for it. Then I'll make a joke like, "And that kid is probably just like me and that's why he doesn't like me." So I can tease and it doesn't really hurt my feelings, it can't. Traditionally—and this is the one thing that stands out over, above, and beyond all my evaluations—I have a good rapport with kids.

Making Connections with the Teacher's Life

I'm good at making connections to my own life that are real. I have two sons; I tell stories about them. All the kids can relate to that. I know when kids tell me about their families and their neighborhood and how embarrassed they are: "Police came to so and so's house," sometimes they'll be screaming at each other, "and the police took his dad away."

I'll say, "It's awful, huh?" because the little boy is embarrassed, and I'll say, "They did that to my brother and I was really embarrassed, but I didn't do it, so why did I feel embarrassed?" The kids hook into that, "Why should he feel embarrassed? He didn't do it." I start connecting with all that.

They basically have to trust me to know that I wouldn't b.s. them, because I wouldn't. If I did, I would tell them, "That's just b.s." Basically that's how I am, I'm a really bottom-line kind of person.

Working in Groups and Winning

I have the kids working in groups all the time. I threw my desks out years ago. Now I have big kidney-shaped tables, those reading tables with five kids to a table. They change groups mathematically, so it's not by chance. The first time it's by chance, except that for the very first time I seed it with one good reader. This will ensure a little bit of success in terms of following directions. Thereafter I just change them diagonally, and then match them up with a new group so that by the end of the year they would have changed about eight or nine times.

They stay in a group about a month, give or take a couple of days, and they get points as a group for good behavior, for doing all the right academic things. For today, I'll say, "I'm going to put up this puzzle. If one of you tells me what you thought about the answer when I did it, I'm going to give your table triple points," and that's a big deal.

The reward for triple points is so piddly: at the end of the month when we all count up our points, that group gets to go out for a free ten-minute recess. There are two tables who can win, because it's no fun for one table to go out on free recess with only five kids. So we have a first-place table and a second-place table. They go out for ten-minute recess, but the first-place tables all get free Glassbrook school pencils. So we give out these piddly prizes.

I think winning is really necessary; maybe it's not winning, but having the sense that you control something that took you from point A to point B and that your behavior helped you to get there. What you did helped you get there. Everyone in my group is going to win before the year is over. I jot down who hasn't won. Before the end of the year, everyone will get an award for academic achievement, for diplomacy, or creativity. So I think that to win is important, also, because then you have to consider the people who didn't win.

I'll tell you what happens to the people who didn't win. When the kids who did win are out, the people who didn't win are writing me a story or a paragraph or a sentence or a picture about things that they can do in the future in order to win. "What do you have to do to win this?" You can get points for asking me a question, you can think, you can show consideration, all kinds of things in the classroom rules. That's generally what they do, and when they're through doing that the kids are coming back in.

If they're not through, it's OK. It's not homework or a punishment, it's just that these are the things you can do. They hand it to me as it is and I keep it, and I might read some good ideas that stand out above the others. That way, they're not always going to be losing, eventually they will know what to do to win and they will win.

Testing for What?

I can do the best job in the world in my classroom and you can come in and say, "This is wonderful," and none of that would be measured in a test. That's frustrating. I think kids need to know certain things and I think we need to be accountable for at what point they will know it and how much of it they will know, but there has to be a different way.

My own personal test that I do with my kids has more to do with understanding and process. "Let's see what you remember. Let's see if you understand why it happened. If you don't, don't worry about it, we'll do it again later." Kids really get scared when there's a test. "But you didn't tell us there was a test." "Well, who cares?"

"What did you do yesterday?" "Well, we popped some popcorn." "Why do you think that kernel of corn popped?" I don't want to know why it popped, I want to know what they think, and so they write about it. One really bright little girl said the kernel of corn popped because it got hot and it couldn't stand it anymore. That's kind of sensible. But scientifically that isn't my point. If they didn't get it, we have time, we'll go back, and we'll do it again.

You're talking to a teacher in a low-achieving school based on our CAP [California Assessment Program] tests.[3] Of course, I don't teach 3rd grade but I can't wash my hands of it because I get my kids ready for 3rd grade. Gosh, I am not sure that testing is the answer. It's an exclusive thing, it excludes many people from getting things they want. It's divisive; how can I put it?

Questioning, and Recognizing Mentors in Teaching

My principal, Marcos, was my mentor. When he hired me—it was really a good interview—he was running down the hall after some kid at La Vista. He was the principal there. I was a mom, going to school; I think I was teaching 2nd grade then, as a sub. He was yelling, "Grace, do you want a job?" I said, "Sure, where?" He said, "I don't know." I said, "What grade?" He said, "I don't know," and I said, "I'll take it." That was my interview. (I was later interviewed formally.)

He felt always that he could put something in my lap and that I would run with it. Marcos is a great man for having ideas; he always gives them to someone else and then sees what they'll do. I remember my first year, going to his office all the time and just saying, "This is what I'm doing or not doing." If he ever felt that I needed help or even modeling, whatever he thought that I needed, he would put me in a situation where it was happening so that I could absorb it, so that I could see it and then he knew that I would do it, and I did. That's what he gave me. I'm still at the same school, teaching 2nd grade now. This is my eighth year at the school, and Marcos' last year here.

Under great duress, stress, and illness he has endured. I've seen him grow too. He used to be a teacher when I was an instructional aide, then he became a principal when I became a teacher, and he just now received his doctorate. He's been assigned to a new position at the district office.

I think he is a real instructional leader; he has been that for me as well as other teachers here. He is very subtle in the way that he gets teachers who have taught for 20 years to learn something new. To my knowledge, he doesn't come out and say "It's new," he becomes inclusive and says, "So and so is doing this. You can be a part of this also."

I do try to take advantage of what's available in the profession. Maybe if I were in a different school, I would have problems in getting what I need, and see what's missing in resources and inservices. I don't know, I haven't been anywhere else where I didn't have access to these things. With Marcos, if I present a legitimate reason and a way for it to ripple out to extend the benefits—that's kind of the secret of it—I can probably get it or do it.

Staff Development and Pay

Staff development [continuing education for teachers] is something I have my eye on, and there's a reason for that. If I haven't gotten something I wanted, it was because of the people in charge of staff development, or the people that I have to go through to get to this end point. So, yes, I have had obstacles in that direction.

When I wanted to present Complex Instruction, I wanted to get paid for the work in the summertime. They didn't want to pay the amount that I was asking; my other two partners didn't really care if they got paid or not. "Let's just do it." Then I said, "No, I think we should be paid." I made a lot of people have a lot of meetings because I insisted that we three get paid. At this point it was an issue, because if I could make money during the summer, I would. I had to; I had two kids and I'm a single mom. Money was an issue, and so was intense preparation time. In the final analysis they paid us, but unprofessional things were said.

Reality, and Public Support

When you order books for a California classroom, the state tells you that there are 24.5 students in each classroom. I have never been in a class that has that few kids, and I would like the state to acknowledge that.

I would also like to see the district administration not make issues a case of "them against us." They always say, "We're in this together" and every year at the beginning of the year they say, "We're looking forward to a great year working with you." They always talk like that, but when it really gets down to issues, it does feel like them against us.

Why am I having to present to the district the reasons why they should give us [bilingual teachers] a stipend? Why didn't they think of it and give it to us? Why didn't they dream it up to get more good bilingual teachers? If they really meant what they said, it would have been their idea.

For our administrators—gosh, I've had such a wonderful administrator—I would like them to be able to do what they ask us to do. I hate it when people tell me to do something that I know they can't do.

So I would like for them to be realistic in their expectations of teachers, given what we have to work with. For example, they send us to a wonderful workshop on manipulatives or on literature, and then we come back to a classroom that's poor in literature materials and in manipulatives [e.g., beans, blocks, toothpicks]. Now, this is the second year I've had manipulatives provided for my classroom. Prior to that I was buying most of them or making them, and this year I can really go to a box and get something I need. Still there's a lot more to be added, we need a lot more things. I want them to give us inservice and the materials to work with and the time to do it.

I would like for them to follow through when they start a program, not just give it to you and walk away from it. Or give it to you and say, "OK," and then some teachers will do it and some won't, and some will do it well, some will do it poorly. I would like some more follow-through.

What Teachers Need from the School Board

I wish the school board would work closer with the teachers and not be divisive, which I think they are, particularly during a bargaining year. That shouldn't be the point; it should be that both groups of people are happy. Last year was like that. The teachers asked for x amount of raise; they got it without any quibble—well maybe some—but they didn't drag it on into the year like they have in the past. Everybody was happy.

We can see the difference in the schools and the teachers that aren't hassled, and don't have to waste all this time doing "hours only," which is always a pain. "Hours only" happens when there is bargaining going on and the contract hasn't been settled. The union will say, "Work hours only." That means that you go in at the exact minute your contract starts; you go in en masse and you leave together the minute your contract hours are up. Nobody wins. Only half your job is done, but you've got to go.

Not Knowing the Kid's Name

I'll probably teach 15 years now just because that's how long it will take me to prepare to do something new. One day I was in the office and a teacher brought in this student—this is January or February, the kid's been in there a while—and said, "I don't want this child in my room any more, he's being disruptive." The secretary said, "What's his name?" The teacher said, "I don't know. I have 32 kids in there."

She was either so upset that she didn't know or she really didn't know. I thought, "God help me that I won't teach to that point." I don't feel anywhere near that point, so that's OK, but I remember that moment. It's frozen in my brain forever like a few things in your life are. This woman didn't know the kid's name.

Family Intervention, and Some Consequences

I have intervened in family situations a couple of times, the first time because the young boy was getting hurt. I reported that; I'm legally bound to. The agencies who take over—then it's out of your hands—took all those four or five kids in his family away. They separated them, either by twos or by ones; they were all separated until the authorities could deal with this problem. I felt—and maybe I still do, I don't know—I felt at that time that the trauma that those kids had from being separated into all these other homes (one of the little girls said, "They smoked all the time") was more harmful to them than the slap this kid had received, or whatever his dad had done.

The boy came to my class with five fingerprints on his face, and that wasn't the first time. He had other issues at other times, and so I reported that. The mom felt so powerless: she couldn't get her kids, the husband had lost his temper, it wasn't even in her control, and she was being punished too, you see? I thought, "I'm never going to report anything again." I felt awful. Another time I reported it and it was taken care of. This year I reported something and I don't think the mom is upset with me so much as she is with the system.

I hate to report unless I'm really really positive that something good will come of it. I've talked to the kids too about that, and we've talked about foster homes. One little girl in my class went to a foster home and she told the other kids what it's like, and she even told the other kids why she went to a foster home, which is a pretty brave thing to do.

Offering Parenting Information, not Indignation

Aside from the reporting that we are legally bound to do [concerning danger to children], I always have to fight with myself so I don't become indignant toward these parents. It's easy to feel self-righteous, and that isn't the point of it. You become judgmental, "Well, why don't you get up and feed your kids breakfast?" or "Why don't you...?"

I wasn't a perfect parent and I'm still not a perfect parent. I think that's what I'm always fighting: not to become judgmental or indignant with these people as though I know all the answers and they don't. I usually offer them information like, "If you need help with parenting, these are courses that you can do"; or, " If you need counseling for yourself or your child, this is the place to go." And I tell them where to go to get protective help for mothers that are abused.

Cal State Hayward is offering classes this spring: "How to get your kid to get perfect grades in math," or "Straight A's in spelling," and parenting classes. I suggested that the PTA sponsor a parent and that our staff sponsor somebody, so that they can go as partners; or Marcos can send one of us. Then we could come back and replicate this whole series on Parent Night at Glassbrook so that we can disseminate all the information in the cheapest way possible. He didn't get back to me yet but he put it in the newsletter, the staff bulletin. I wouldn't be the best person to send. I think he should send a teacher who had little ones at home still, so that would benefit that teacher plus whatever could be brought back.

Parents, Homework, and Portfolios of Writing

I also talk to parents in my report cards: "We're working on writing a paragraph. Your child needs to study math facts at home for five minutes an evening." One mother said, "He only had five math problems last night." But that's all it takes. Five every night. I'd go nuts if somebody gave me 50 to do at once.

I have a portfolio for each student, so once or twice a month we write something, we give it a title, and we stick it in the folder. In June when they take the portfolio home they're going to see that their very first paper was an example of their alphabet. I want to know who has reversals [of letters], who doesn't, who knows the alphabet, and a sample of writing from one to 100. Testing in my classroom happens only when it's absolutely required. Who knew it and who didn't? As kids come in, they're tested with the same paper that we're doing at this level right now. At the end of the year, we can look at the beginning and see how much they've grown.

I also have standards sheets; I have an example of a good paragraph written by an average 2nd grader. So when a mother says, "Why did my kid get this grade?" I'll pull out the kid's page and compare it. I'll say, "There are 30 kids in here and let's say 18 of them can write like this. This is the standard that your child is facing, and this is the standard that he's being measured by. Now, if your child came in and had all these reversals in September and now he's writing better, he has his own work to compare."

When the Parent is a Problem

I've had a couple of discipline problems, but usually it's the parent that's the problem, not the child. I'm really worried right now because I have one mom who is a problem. Just from watching what's going on she probably thinks I hate her child, but I'm nuts about him because he's a wonderful human being. He's funny and he's considerate and he's warm and he's loving. I want to give him an award for being funny, mostly, but I can't because his funniness makes him get in trouble with the rest of the class. I figure down the road a little bit, if he matures a little and he sees what a gift it is to make people laugh, I can reward him for that.

He is in a bilingual class. The bilingual classes are different, in that in the morning I have all the Spanish-readers and in the afternoon I have all the English-readers. This mother wants me to babysit her boy for an hour a day, although I don't think she would say that. She is convinced that her child can read in both languages, and that if he can't, then I should keep him so that he does. I said, "I won't force the transition on a child. I let the child develop into that transition, and if I see a readiness I'd be the first one to start him in English reading because it's advantageous." It wasn't such a bad thing that she wanted this for her child, but I tried to tell her that he really wasn't ready. He's having trouble in both languages. I'm not sure if it's behavioral or developmental or what with him, but he just is.

She said, "But my other child goes at this time, what am I going to do? Go home and come back and go home and come back?" I'm sitting there saying, "Well, gee, that really is a problem. Maybe you could find a friend who walks home at the same time." I really did try to help her in a nice way.

This parent took the kid to Chicago for four weeks; this kid who's already struggling, who doesn't need not to be in school, has gone on vacation. Then she comes back and wants me to keep him all day. At that point he didn't fit my English reading group any more. We had just taken off. Finally they made a decision that we could all live with. I said, "OK, if she would rather have him in English reading than in Spanish reading, we'll do that." I think it's a big mistake and I told all three of them that.

I thought, "This poor mother must think I hate her kid, because I hassle her so much," but it isn't that. It's just that what is best for the kid is not what the adults are choosing.

Parents Should Question Teachers

My own parents would never question my teachers. They would always do what the teachers said and believe what they said because they said it. I question my kids' teachers. If somebody tries to give me a line about "Mr. So-and-So is really an excellent teacher, and we don't know why you want to pull your child from his class," I say, "Pull him or I'll go above you," because I know. Then I have to apologize, because I say, "I know it's your job to protect this person." If somebody spoke to Marcos about me, he would be supportive of me.

But if we continue to protect people who aren't doing their jobs, or who are abusing or disempowering kids, well then maybe there's not much to be said for teaching as a profession.

A Safe Place to Grow

I would like parents to trust that I am doing the best I can, and for them to provide a place for their kids to do the work I send home; and a place to be safe. If a kid comes to me because somebody at home is all messed up, or all these horrendous things are happening, then whatever I have to say is only going to half-happen, or partially happen.

I'm not saying that parents should believe everything I have to say, because obviously I don't have all the answers, and not everybody is like me; but they should definitely provide, to the best of their ability, a safe place for this kid to grow. It would seem like such a simple thing to happen.

The Union Rep: I'll Do It

I've always been politicized—kind of a muckraker. I always ask the questions that nobody wants to ask but everybody's thinking.

One of my professors taught me to challenge the sacred cows and not feel bad about it; to stand up and say, "But why are you doing this when this is obviously wrong or this could be better? It could be changed." I think that maybe I lacked polish or I lacked a process for doing that, and so a lot of times I would be in trouble for saying things.

I am active in the union. At our school, the reading specialist was the union rep. She had been doing the work for a couple of years and asked me to do it. I was saying, "I don't have time, I'm doing all these other things." Finally last year, at the staff meeting, they said, "We need a new rep for next year." I looked around; I'm the kind of person who, when everybody waits, waits the longest. I said, "I'll do it."

That was two years ago; I started going to the meetings of the HEA (Hayward Education Association). It's part of NEA (National Education Association), and CTA (California Teachers Association).

Bilingual Teachers' Group

I became the rep because nobody else would, basically. Teachers had been trying to get me to come to meetings. They had been trying to form a bilingual teachers' group and they were saying that bilingual teachers had different agendas and different needs that had to be addressed at HEA meetings, and that no one was speaking for us.

As part of my travels and looking around for another place, possibly, to live, I found out that many other districts paid bilingual teachers stipends for being bilingual. The stipends were from $1,000 extra a year to 5 percent of your income, depending on where the need was or what district it was. After many boring meetings at HEA, I decided to go to a meeting of these teachers who had gotten together. They met with the president of HEA and she gave us a structure for our future meetings and our planning.

We decided to propose for the new bargaining year that bilingual teachers get a stipend for being bilingual. I was not really a part of that first year because I was just getting into it. They managed to get $200 a year above our salary, which was like a joke, an insult, if you will. That got me mad, and once it got me mad I wanted to do something about it, and so I went to the meeting. Some lady said, "We really should make them double it, or make it $500," and I said, "No. Why bother? Ask them for $1,500. It's not high and it's not low, it's reasonable."

We had a planning committee and we decided that we would get all the salaries of other districts, and give our proposal some organization. I would present first to the HEA board, to all the people there, the representatives from all the schools, and then I would present to the school board. Now, everyone had ideas for what should go in there, but somebody thought that I had a lot of gall to ask for $1,500 after a lousy $200 a year. I felt that if they weren't going to ask for this that I didn't want to participate, because then I would feel like, "What a useless act."

The Politics of Presentation

We went ahead and did it, presented to the HEA board, and I kind of braced myself. I brought people who were bilingual to this meeting where I was going to speak. It was a time of confusion for lots of other groups that were speaking because they were not very well organized; whatever their project was, it wasn't well articulated.

Finally it was my turn and I got to talk about all the different things that we do as bilingual teachers that a regular teacher doesn't do. We had made a list. We talked about how we helped kids who have reading problems because there are no reading specialists that are bilingual. We have to deal a lot with our kids who have to be referred for special education because there were no special education programs for bilingual kids. We have to translate a lot of material; everything that goes up on the bulletin board has to go up twice, in two languages. Sometimes it's just the time involved.

Of course, the president said, "So, what is it you want?" I said, "Well, I would like for us to ask for $1,500 more a year as a stipend. As you can see, it's not the lowest and it's not the highest. Basically that's it." I had talked with a woman who was not a bilingual teacher—because this is where the power comes in—and asked her to make the motion. So a non-bilingual teacher made the motion that this be put on our bargaining agenda and a bilingual teacher seconded it. All but one person voted for it.

Now, you have to know about me, that I didn't even care about the money. With me it was an issue. I didn't even care if it was bargained off the table. I thought, "This is fantastic. You know, you're talking about people who had always talked bad about bilingual education." Afterwards, everybody came and said, "Oh, you really did a good job." Well, I just said the words; a lot of people wrote them. It was a good feeling.

A week or so later I spoke to the school board and basically said the same thing. Afterwards two board members came and asked me to make time to talk to them a little more about it. (The board meeting is every quarter so I'm sure they had all the information anyway.) It went through without a hitch. We got the stipend. It was really great. I would have never cared if we did or didn't win, because I'd been working all those years without it anyway. With me it was just the fact that all these people supported it.

The people at HEA said it was nice to hear something that was developed and presented and that they could make a clean decision about. So anyway, we did get it and I was really jazzed. That's the kind of stuff that motivates me, not just for the association but anything that I'm involved in. I have a certain amount of patience for change; then if it doesn't happen, I'll leave. Or if I have a project, I'll hang in there and see it through, and then I'll move on.

School Politics, and Good Rapport

Establishing good rapport is everyone's responsibility. There are instances where one teacher dislikes another teacher because of something she did ten years ago, or other things: "She never brings treats." Or "He never does his yard duty on time." I said to somebody one day, "Gosh, your life must be so perfect that you pick at this piddly stuff."

I overheard one day that somebody thought that Marcos gave preferential treatment to bilingual teachers. It wasn't meant for my ears so I conducted myself as I always have—as if I hadn't heard it. I look back and I think, "No, I think he doesn't treat the person with a preference, he treats the program with a preference. This is his issue in life."

He has hired Afghani-speaking instructional aides. He brought in one Afghani professor to speak to us about the escape he had gone through to get here, and the circuitous route that he had to take. It was really an adventure story. So Marcos doesn't just address the Spanish bilingual issues, he addresses all the differences.

The good rapport our teachers have, I think, is based on everybody wanting to have a good school, and so when we become divided by minor issues, the big picture comes back and then we get united again.

New Faces At Glassbrook School

I've gone through a photographic history of Hayward's Glassbrook School in the teachers' lounge, where they have all those old photographs from the 50s and 60s. All those little kids looked like the cast from "Leave It to Beaver"— nice little crew cuts, cute little striped shirts. Everybody was Anglo, maybe one or two brown faces, not a lot.

Then somewhere, the color started to change, the kind of kid started to change. If you were to compare a Glassbrook picture today to one of those, it would be like you had moved to another place on the earth because the structure of the community changed.

The profession has changed in the 15 years I have been in it. I do feel positive about teaching. My whole perception of teaching was like Miss Landers, you know, from the Beaver Cleaver days. The teacher always dressed a certain way and spoke a certain way, and had a lot of reserve. You could get so far, and that's it.

I see a real openness now. Teachers are looked at more as individuals, and teachers are being more involved with the parents. Our staff is divided into three. One group has been there 23 years or more; the middle group has been there eight to ten years; and then there's one group of people who have been there one or two years. You can almost see the differences in the way kids are dealt with and the way problems are dealt with.

Views of Bilingual Education

The bilingual program started at this school with Marcos' first day as a principal and my first day as a teacher, and nobody liked it. "We don't want it here. There's no need. The kids have been fine all these years." That kind of an attitude. He said, "Well, this is my task and it's going to get done." The bilingual program had a legal base: if you have x number of children who speak a language, you must teach them in their dominant language. Glassbrook long ago had these numbers and had qualified for a bilingual program but wasn't getting it.

You can imagine how you might feel if you've been teaching a class for 10 or 15 years, and you've been used to one kind of community. Little by little it's been changing, and nobody's said, "It's changing. We need this or that." Marcos comes in with a new program, and some of your best friends have to go to another school because the new program has displaced them. There are a lot of personal feelings, a lot of misunderstandings and antagonisms toward the program, maybe not toward the people, but the people absorb that because of the program. I certainly did my first year there.

I'm not sure that it was a personal issue, because I'm this kind of person: I like to get to know people and I like people, period. When people would want to talk about the philosophical issues about bilingual education or about the intellectual issues of bilingual ed, I had been so used to it at that point that I felt fully armed to say this, this, and this about bilingual education, and "Your acceptance or non-acceptance is not my concern, so let's not make that an issue."

I started here in a 1st grade bilingual class, and I'm still in a bilingual program in whatever grade I teach. During the eight years I've been teaching bilingual classes, some people's attitudes have improved, because they've seen the "why" of it. For some, it hasn't changed, but they're not really vocal. Another thing that's happened at Glassbrook is that the staff has changed. We've had some people retire, some people transfer in, and we have a lot of first-year teachers, a lot of new teachers.

The program had evolved from a 50/50 composition, where the English-speaking kids learned Spanish and the Spanish-speaking kids learned English; this is what I used to have at my other school. That program phased out.

Most of the kids at Glassbrook who spoke Spanish would continue to learn in Spanish, but it was not a maintenance program. We would move them into English as best we could, to help them become fluent quickly. They used to imply a deadline, to speak English by 3rd grade or 4th grade or whatever, but Marcos never put a grade on it. Our intent was to give service to those kids who were already there and needed the bilingual program and weren't getting it.

Hazards of Teachers' Own Agendas

It's a good assumption that a bilingual program means an implicit acceptance of the child. It would stand to reason, but that isn't always the case. Sometimes you get people from South America who become bilingual teachers, and they have their own little built-in agenda about racism and prejudice. Sometimes you get Anglo teachers who don't speak Spanish as a first language. Teachers come with their own agendas. The way people are disempowered is covert, it's not out there.

There's a bilingual teacher from Spain that I had an opportunity to talk to at a bilingual conference. We were talking about how to empower Hispanic parents to be a part of the school and let them know that they are their children's first teachers; and how to help them grow in literature, and open communication between them and their children. You want these parents to feel the freedom to come to school, you want to accept their culture, you want to accept their families.

This woman from Spain said—and I believe she felt it, she lived it—"How can you accept that? These people are uncultured." This woman was in a classroom with little Latino kids. She was not in there with Spanish kids. There's a big difference.

Another woman who was a teacher of mine at Cal State had gone so far as to dye her hair blonde. She was light in complexion. She said that in South America if you had blonde hair and light skin you were treated better and dealt with in higher circles, because otherwise you were considered Indian.

Why should you learn to speak English quickly? Why should you keep Spanish? Why not just discard it? A lot of people are too embarrassed to speak Spanish, even if they are in a bilingual classroom. I do a lot of feedback to bilingual kids. "Raise your hand if you're bilingual." I tell them, "Did you know that I wouldn't be here standing and talking to you if I weren't bilingual? I would have never been hired as an instructional aide, I would have never been hired to be a teacher, if I hadn't spoken Spanish." I bring in Spanish poetry and literature, and I let them know that this stuff has been translated into other languages.

Who Succeeds?

The attitude of some people toward the bilingual program was, "You've always learned English without this program, what's the problem now? Look at you. You're a teacher, you never had bilingual education. Why do these kids need it?" The answer to that is, "Yes, I am a teacher, but it took me a long time to become a teacher. I didn't go the normal route, number one. Number two is, I'm a teacher out of 12 kids in my family who are not professional people. I'm a high school graduate out of 12 kids in my family, where only two of us graduated from high school. So it has a lot to say about me as a strong individual who kept pursuing in spite of it all. No one should have to fight that hard to get there. Most people don't.

"Yes, I did it. But look at all these other people who didn't and who still can't, for whatever reasons. I don't think it's an accident that nine of my surviving brothers and sisters dropped out of high school and the two of us didn't—which isn't to say that they didn't go back and become late bloomers like myself, because some of them did." I'm right in there with the statistics. A few succeed, but for the most part, many don't.The bilingual program gives more kids a better chance to stay in school.

Celebrations at Our House

All the students in my bilingual class are not native Spanish speakers. I have a healthy mixture of kids. I have some Anglo children; this year I have a lot of African American kids, which is neat, because in the past I only had one or two. The kids have racial issues, but I haven't seen them in the classroom. You might see them on the playground. I think the only racial slur that was ever made was by one African American kid to another in my class, but I never see it among my students as a put-down to somebody else.

We talk about multi-cultural ideas but I don't give it a name. We did a paper, "I know it's Thanksgiving at my house because" and then they had to write all the stuff that was happening at their homes. We read the papers aloud to each other and talk about how we're all kind of doing the same thing with a different twist to it. Something else we wrote about was, "You should have been at my birthday party." They write down a whole bunch of things that they did at their birthday parties. Some kids have a piñata, some don't. Some kids go to Baxter's [restaurant], some visit grandpa. We talk about how different people celebrate birthdays, and how in my family we celebrated our saint's day and that sort of thing.

I always start out with my family, I always say something about my mom and dad, even discipline. "When I was a kid I got spanked for doing ... and don't you just hate that?" Then all the kids say, "Yeah." They want to tell you everything that happens to them and then some; so, that's kind of how I deal with it.

Both Respect and Skepticism

When my mother passed away, many of the people at the funeral treated me with such respect. They were first-generation Mexican families. Whenever I am in a group of Latino people and they find out I'm a teacher, I get so much respect that I feel humble. I feel like, "I don't really deserve this. I'm just this crazy woman, so cut it out." I'm embarrassed by it, see? But doctors and lawyers are not embarrassed when they get societal respect. They feel that it's their due, and I think teachers need to feel that way.

In other places, I've been in a social situation where people have come up and said, "When are you guys [teachers] going to start teaching our kids anything?" and I've had to say, "Come to my classroom and you'll see who's learning." I can only go by me.

Notes

[1] A system for classifying educational objectives. See Benjamin S. Bloom (ed.), *Taxonomy of Educational Objectives: Cognitive Domain* (NY: David McKay, 1956).

[2] For a description of the Complex Instruction program, see Elizabeth G. Cohen, *Designing Groupwork: Strategies for the Heterogeneous Classroom* (NY: Teachers' College Press, 1986).

[3] The California Assessment Program (CAP) is a statewide assessment program aimed at evaluating school performance and is given to students in grades 3, 6, 8, and 12.

Part 2

INSIDE THE CLASSROOM AND THE PROFESSION

When some of the smallest children first venture into school, they may believe that their teacher lives exclusively in the classroom and only for the purpose of teaching them.[1] Adults, who know more about the real lives of teachers, smile at the children's view, but in their own way the children have found a truth they and others may in time forget. The classroom is a center of life.

Quality teaching and learning shapes, enlarges, and sometimes saves lives. The classroom may be small, and the number of students too large, but when the teacher and the students get to work, the possibilities are far from trivial. The way the teacher learns to teach and connect with children is one element of the profession; another is the way the teacher functions and learns to connect with colleagues.

Exchanging ideas and experiences with other teachers is a critical mode of growth. Good teachers can generate their own professional energies, but even the best of them need to talk and plan with colleagues to break out of their isolation, try different ideas, and learn from each other. Professionalism grows exponentially, when teachers like Suzy Ronfeldt and Elois Irvin can teach and learn with colleagues.

Suzy Ronfeldt

Elois Irvin

Suzy Ronfeldt: The Teacher and the Classroom—How to Learn, How to Live

Finding the Balance: The Art of Teaching

The longer I teach, the closer I come to finding the right balance between my setting the stage and being a facilitator of the children's learning, and having them be independent thinkers and decision-makers. The longer I teach, the closer I come to simplifying the curriculum to a couple of big goals in each subject and narrowing the number of activities, so children have time to raise and answer their own questions.

I have been teaching 5th grade for eight years in Albany now and I still revise and rethink what I'll do each day as if it were my first year.* My husband gets upset with me because I spend so much time changing what I'm doing. In a way, I get upset with myself. I think that is part of the whole creative process I like about teaching. I'm fascinated with it. I write notes to myself all the time with ideas on how to extend an activity for the following year. Of course, the real test is to find the notes again when I need them.

In this kind of organic teaching where I am creating the curriculum, it is crucial that I am organized and can put my hands on my thoughts, my plans, my rethinking for each concept or activity in each subject.

At the beginning of this school year, I tried talking into a tape recorder to help me as a teacher-researcher, but when was I going to find time to listen to the tapes? I'd give anything to get a grant to have someone in education researching my classroom day. Then that person and I could discuss what went on, what the children were thinking, where we should go from here, how I could have listened longer or asked the right question. In this way, I could fine-tune this art—the art of teaching.

---

*In Fall 1990, the Albany City Unified School District enrolled 2,464 students and employed 177 teachers in 3 elementary schools, 1 middle school, and 1 comprehensive high school. The student demographics were: 12.2% African American; 20% Asian; 1.3% Filipino; 9.6% Hispanic; 1% Native American; 1.3% Pacific Islander; and 54.6% White. Four percent of the families were on AFDC.

The Community of Whitefish, Montana

I grew up in Whitefish, Montana, a town of 5,000. My father had a lot to do with starting the ski area. To supplement his teaching income, he coached several sports, including skiing, for the high school. Our family friends were the editor of the paper and the town doctor, but our closest friends were people who worked on the ski slopes and on the railroad. These people were genuine and real. They were not pretentious. Everyone knew one another and I always felt the warm support of people beyond my own family.

My best friend, Nancy, was raised in a Japanese internment camp in Heart Mountain, Wyoming. Her family had been moved there from the Stockton area during World War II. Nancy never talked about this indignity, but every year my class and I read *Journey Home* by Yoshiko Uchida and spend a month studying this period of United States history. I do this in honor of her family, the Muraokas.

I did not feel that I got a particularly solid academic foundation in school. Most of it was very textbook oriented. I was basically the kind of student who memorized her way through and was rewarded highly for that. My father was very good about not being critical of other teachers, yet I knew his philosophy of education and we talked about it frequently. He had come a long way from being a rote textbook teacher whose students were fully prepared for multiple-choice college entrance exams, to being a hands-on, open kind of classroom teacher who valued thinking over memorizing.

By the time I left for college, my father was a real maverick. When he became superintendent, he designed and had built an elementary school that had pods and open classrooms. He pursued his beliefs about education even though half of his faculty was upset about his liberal ideas. Today, the school bears his name.

The Big World of College

I went to Whitman College, in Walla Walla, Washington, which was the closest liberal arts college I could find. My folks wanted me to go East where there were geographical scholarships for students from Montana, but I had a steady boyfriend in Montana, and I wanted to be as close as I could. Walla Walla was large to me. The college was absolutely beautiful, and for the first time in my life, I was with other students who were all interested in getting a college degree. I found this truly stimulating.

I was stretched a lot more than I had been in high school. It wasn't just "rote, fill-in-the-blanks" kind of work any longer. I had to reason and think

through my own position on things. For the first time, I had to write to
express my ideas, not to regurgitate what someone else told me. I also had
fun in college. I decided to enter Whitman, where nobody knew me, with a
less studious image, so I went by Suzy instead of Mary. I am still called Mary
by my friends in Montana. My real name is Mary Suzanne.

My Father Was My Role Model

I was in college in the early 60s before there were a lot of professional
options for women. I was thinking in terms of becoming a teacher or nurse; I
did not want to be a secretary. My father was a high school chemistry and
physics teacher for some 30 years, and he was my role model in many, many
ways.

I knew I was going to be getting married; I knew I was going to have a
family, and it seemed like teaching would fit into my 1950s-60s expectations
of life. I had always secretly wanted to be an architect but didn't think that
was possible for me. My father and I together designed the family's cabin on
the lake in Montana and we had birch trees growing through the living
room. I was fascinated with setting up rooms and designing space for living.

I was the eldest of three children. My mother did not work when we were
little. My father was happy in his profession. It was hard financially for us,
but we had so many things. We lived in a small town; we were able to go
skiing on the weekend and in the summer we lived on a nearby lake, so even
on my father's limited salary we had a lot of options. When I was ready to go
to college it was a real concern how my parents were going to pay for it. I
was a good student and they wanted me to be able to go to a private school.

When I left for college in 1960, my father became superintendent of schools
partly to help pay for my education. When he made this move, his salary
rose from $5,000 to $8,000. When he retired as superintendent in 1971, he
was earning $15,000. Now he is 84 years old and he and my mother live on a
retirement pay based on that income.

Teaching in a Country School

By the time I was a junior at Whitman College, I was seriously dating my
husband Steve and, after graduation, I followed him to Berkeley,
California—the last place any decent Montana girl should go.

While Steve attended Boalt Hall School of Law at Cal [University of California at Berkeley], I taught out in the Mt. Diablo Unified School District in a little school in Pacheco. At that time, 1964, it was out in the country.

The personnel manager of the school district was from Montana, and I got the job via the telephone. He placed me there and I was delighted because there were horses and pastures and open space. It reminded me of home. In those days you could get a teaching certificate with only a Bachelor of Arts degree and you didn't major in education. I was a history major.

I vividly remember one pivotal moment in that 4th grade classroom when we were talking about tornadoes. The children did not get it until one little girl suddenly suggested we go to the sink and watch the water go down the drain to get an idea of the swirling motion and power of tornadoes. She was excited about her wonderful idea and the children understood much better from this concrete model. It was a magical moment and I vowed then and there to set up a classroom where children had more opportunities to share their own understandings with the rest of us.

A Job to Provide for Three Children

After a year, Steve and I were married and I began to teach in the Richmond Unified School District. I taught there for two years until he finished law school. Right away I was pregnant, had our first child, and quit teaching. At that time, I was eager to be a mother and be at home. My husband was a poverty lawyer and still is in Oakland, so we were not making big money, but I loved being home. I took out my State Teachers' Retirement money and we bought our first house. We had three children within four and a half years and it was a special time in my life. I didn't plan to go back to work as a teacher until the children were grown.

Soon after the birth of our third child, my husband was diagnosed with melanoma. We were both 30 years old. When your spouse has cancer, you realize that you may have to provide for the children on your own. I made a decision that I'd have to further my education to be higher on the pay scale, and then I'd get back into teaching. I think if the illness hadn't come along and once the children were all in school, I would have looked at options other than teaching. I had always been interested in architecture, but as it was, I had already taught three years and I did enjoy being in the classroom.

When you have melanoma, you are kind of playing Russian roulette. The doctors give you five years and they can't say if you are going to make it or not. That gave me time while the children were still young, to get my

Masters through an external degree program. I wrote my thesis on "Reading, Writing, and Mathematics Above and Beyond Workbooks and Textbooks."

As soon as my youngest was in kindergarten, I began to work part time as a resource teacher in Richmond. Things were looking pretty good. My husband had lived five years at that point and we were feeling fairly confident that he would not have any further problems with melanoma. (Now it has been 18 years and his fondest wish has been granted: He has lived to share his life intimately with the children and has seen each of them graduate from high school.)

When I tried to re-enter teaching in the 1970s, it was hard because there were no jobs. I wanted desperately to teach in an alternative school in the Berkeley Public Schools, but it was impossible. I had to crawl my way back professionally for the next five or six years. Every year I was laid off, partly because I was a resource person. My position was supported by categorical funds and Richmond Unified never knew from year to year what would happen to the funding.

Resource teachers were the district's safety valve and we often didn't know the day before school started where we would be or what job we would have. One year I would be assigned to K–3 math and reading, and another year to 4–6 math at a different school. As resource teachers, usually we were in math and reading, and sometimes writing.

Learning by Doing

I feel that many of the education courses I had in college and in my Master's program were not valuable. The first course I thought was worthwhile was the Bay Area Writing Project summer session.[2] That experience was like a fresh breeze to me for it was not taught in the traditional way by having an outside expert at the front of the room telling us "how to" teach writing. We were treated as thinking, capable professionals and were involved in "doing" writing right away, then modeling and sharing our own writing with one another in small groups. A BAWP staff member was present in our writing group sessions, but as a facilitator of the discussion, not as a lecturer. The writing and the responding was in our hands. I wrote a special piece on my grandfather that summer and I am still moved when I hear the voice of my Montana childhood come through in sentences such as "watching the moon jump up from behind the mountain," or "drinking buttermilk by letting it gently trickle down the back of the throat."

This has been a wonderful model for me in my own classroom. I treat children as writers and encourage them to work with writing partners or peer editors from among their classmates. They write often and continually share and respond to one another's work. I act as a facilitator. When a child reads a piece with strong similes or metaphors, such as blue whales being called "blue-colored war lords," I point out this writing technique to the children. If another child has used some strong description such as "the clouds that crept through the trees made an eerie shadow on the pine-needle ground," and the children do not pick up on this in their response time, I share the personification I notice with them.

BAWP opened up new vistas for me and my teaching by honoring me as a writer from the first day. Now I do that with my children from the first day of school.

The EQUALS mathematics sessions were another positive experience for me; I was involved with math problems that required me to work through my thinking with concrete materials or diagrams. I was "doing" mathematics activities which were not just tied to numbers. Again, I was not being told how to teach and what to teach. Instead, I was directly involved in the problem solving and explaining my thinking to others in my small group. I was immersed in mathematics as a learner from the first day. I was not asked to do a series of rote tasks in order to get ready for some meaningful problems. Instead, I was involved in the problems right away. My mind was stretched, not stifled—the "aha!" effect.

Finally, my course work with Marilyn Burns' program, The Math Solution, and with the California Math Leadership Program helped me become less focused on the mathematics activity and more focused on my own understanding and thinking strategies.[3]

As a learner, I found I needed time both to work through my own ideas and to hear the thinking of others. Explaining my ideas helped clarify my reasoning. I began to feel I could make sense out of mathematics after all, and I didn't need to memorize someone else's explanation.

In the Math Solution, when we doubled the string circumference of our original circle and found the area was four times as great by drawing on grid paper, I began to get a feeling for the relationship between the radius, the area, and the circumference of a circle. When we halved the string circumference of our original circle and found the area was one fourth the original area, I became more involved in why this was happening. I needed even more time for thinking and reasoning with circles. For too many years, I had been given a formula to memorize and had been robbed of the special excitement that comes from understanding why the formula works. I am determined that my students not be short-circuited in their mathematics learning as I had been. I am determined that they have time to construct their own understandings and have their own "ahas."

What Works: Reflections as Learner, Reflections as Teacher

Although there are many barriers to making a change in the way we teach mathematics [discussed below], there are some positive conditions. First, all of our faculty took the summer Math Solution course together; we were all coming from the same workshop experience where we were actively engaged as learners in rich mathematics problems that crossed all the strands, not just number. We had an opportunity to reflect on our thinking as learners in small groups of four.

Then we had time when teachers of the same grade level were grouped together, to reflect on the mathematics experiences as teachers. This bridge from reflection as learner to reflection as teacher was a meaningful step in the change process. Even our principal took the course, so all of us were speaking from and making decisions from a common ground.

Second, our school had a single focus on mathematics for three years as we worked on a monthly basis with the California Math Leadership Program. Meaningful change involves this kind of time and support. Too often school boards or administrators expect their teachers to focus on two or three different areas each year and to move toward substantial curriculum revision in each. Such unrealistic stretching results in surface change—on paper only—to satisfy state School Improvement Program requirements.

During their monthly visits, the California Math Leadership Program staff, Ruth Parker and Kathy Richardson, provided us with meaningful mathematical experiences and asked us continually to reflect on: 1) our own experiences as learners, 2) the implications for our students' learning of mathematics, and 3) classroom implementation issues. We "did" and we "talked" mathematics.

Time as a Critical Factor

We were given no prescribed program and each of us was the instructional decision-maker for his or her own classroom. This was not easy. Even with all the support the school staff received in concrete materials, summer and on-going staff development over three years, we needed school time to share ideas and to solve problems with our colleagues.

As it was, we had to stay much too late, come much too early, and talk over the weekends on our own time as we tried to develop a year's curriculum for each grade level. Each of us was in a different place with our mathematics thinking and each of us had different feelings about the whole change process. All was not rosy, but I am impressed by the level of mathematics questioning that we now have in our faculty.

I used to believe that a teacher needed only to observe in a classroom where this kind of approach was happening, to have a feeling for what mathematics instruction could be. Then the teacher would take appropriate steps in his or her own classroom. I also used to believe that a series of workshops at the end of the school day could help a teacher change. (I did both of these approaches as a mentor of other teachers.)

Now I realize that time is a critical factor. In our classrooms, we need time to hear and reflect on each child's thinking; time to make next-day decisions based on our assessment of that thinking; time to observe in one another's classrooms; and time to do more reading about learning theory and math activities. We need time to develop grade-level appropriate menus [sequences of activities] with colleagues; time to sit back and appreciate what steps each of us has taken toward a mathematics curriculum that involves students more; and time to make sense out of the meaningful untidiness of our children's mathematical day.

As Albany's class size increases, as Albany's School Board feels more reluctant to allow all-day staff development days for the teachers because of the child-care problem for parents, and as our Wednesday faculty meetings become more structured by district business, where is this necessary time to be found?

Products or Process in Writing

In my classroom, the children do a lot of writing all across the curriculum. When children find their own voices and become playful with their words in expressive writing, they begin to beg for Writers' Workshop time where they get writing-partner response; they revise, then share their pieces about the everyday moments in their lives with the rest of the class. Through writing in math, the children are eager to explain and diagram their own strategies for solving problems such as dividing a triangle into halves, fourths, and eighths, and then proving their thinking. In literature, the children write to make an interpretive point about what the author "means" by using words that the author "says" in the story as proof. Fifth graders are capable of some very high-level thinking and I learn as much from them as they do from me.

One of the mistakes I made as a young writing teacher was that I expected products—products that I could show to parents and products that I could grade. I was more interested in the writing than in the writer. During a five-week summer session with the Bay Area Writing Project, I was immersed in the process of writing. The experience of working with a group and hearing one another's writing was a powerful model I quickly incorporated into my classroom. I no longer wrote all over each child's rough draft "telling" what needed to be done to the piece to make it better. Instead, with a writing partner or during whole-group response time, the child heard what others thought was strong about his or her piece and answered questions about the confusing parts.

Still I continued to assign the writing topics and I did lead the children along by telling them two or three ways to begin a paper and how to clinch a paper by referring back to the lead paragraph. The students' final drafts were impressive products—all in my voice. It was as if each child wrote with me talking into his or her ear.

Then I read *Writing: Teachers and Children at Work* by Donald Graves and *The Art of Teaching Writing* by Lucy Calkins. I was ready to listen to these New England educators. Both of these writing experts suggested that children choose their own writing topics from their own life experiences first, so their words would be a more natural extension of themselves. They also recommended conferring often with a child not by looking at the piece, but by nudging the writer into being a critical reader of her or his own work.

Instead of suggesting, "I think you should add more detail here" and "I think you should move this sentence up there," I do less directing of the piece now. In fact, I don't even look at the piece. I listen as the child reads. Then my questions focus on the writer as thinker, as decision-maker. I might ask questions to help the words flow. "What else happened at the baseball park?" or "Why did you want to write about this moment in your everyday life?" Another question might deal with process. "What do you plan to do next with this piece?"

The children and I have Writers' Workshop three mornings a week and it is an exciting time when we hear each others' wonderful words as our voices come through loud and clear. After about six weeks, we begin to notice aspects of strong writing; we start our classroom list: humor, balance between dialogue and narrative, painted word pictures, similes, vivid verbs. Then I do mini-lessons around these points. Writing skills such as the use of quotation marks or capital letters are taught individually in the context of an editing conference on final draft pieces only.

Each child has a "Little Red Writing Folder" where all the rough drafts are kept as well as an on-going topic list. Some rough drafts are left to bake a long time and some never make it to final draft. During the beginning semester of 5th grade, children need to take a piece to final draft only about once a month. They decide which one, and they explain "what I think is strong about the piece" and "what I would change if I were going to write another draft."

Children as Publishers

Each year, we publish two or three books. Usually one is a book of their poetry, another is a book of their favorite final draft pieces, and another includes their diary entries as they cross the Oregon Trail in class for three weeks each Spring. Lately the children have been doing their own word processing on these books using MultiScribe on our classroom Apple IIe. This is quite a feat since we have only one or two computers for 30 students.

Every year each class picks a publishing company name and logo. This year the students chose "Shake, Rattle, and Write" because of the Loma Prieta earthquake on October 17th. Other publishing names have been Cetacean Corporation (we studied whales a great deal that year), Cool Kids Corporation, United Student Authors (a patriotic group), and Inkpot Press.

The Issue of Tracking

My first four years in Albany, we switched subjects every hour of the morning because we tracked for reading and we tracked for math [grouping children by perceived ability levels]. I'm not that kind of teacher. I was going crazy because we'd be involved in something exciting and meaningful then suddenly we'd have to cut it off to switch subjects and children. There was no meaningful flow to the year.

Finally, I was able to convince my colleagues to try untracking math, then the next year, reading. If we hadn't, I would have switched schools or grade levels. Too often the so-called top track children were into quick right answers in mathematics. During our first untracked year when we also did more cooperative learning, some parents felt their children were just helping others to learn. They felt their children might be losing out and they missed being able to say "My Sally is in the top math group."

I had to talk about several of the positive aspects of non-tracked classrooms. First of all, when a child has to explain her thinking and reasoning so another child understands it, she clarifies her thoughts and really learns what she is trying to teach. Second, you begin to realize that each child has his or her own way of conceptualizing. Third, if you are able to put yourself in the other person's shoes and see how he thinks and interprets, your own understanding is enriched.

In a classroom that honors children's thinking and problem solving, tracking is too narrowing. How do you track children as they try to figure out which is longer—the length of the 5th grade hall or the height of the school building? As my class worked in groups of four on this problem one of them had posed, they arrived at a rich variety of strategies.

One group used the large outside blocks on the building to figure the height. Another group used string tied to a piece of tanbark and threw it from one roof level to another to measure the height. Another group got hold of the blueprints for the building. Still another group measured the two levels of stairs using each step to figure some of the building height. Another group simply went outside and held their hands as blinders on each side of their head then sighted in on the length of the hall, turned their heads and sighted in on the height of the building. The last group took down the architect's drawing from the office wall and measured the length and height from that. Do you label one of these strategies as the "gifted" approach or are they all "gifted" approaches?

In Albany, I have not had questions about tracking from the parents in the last three years. They seem to feel their children are being challenged.

Choosing Partners for Cooperative Learning

I used to agonize over how I group my students in teams of four or five. It was such an involved process that I had the children switch only every six to eight weeks. They each listed two or three choices of people they'd like to work with. I used a sociogram as I tried to give each child at least one of the choices, and attempted to balance each group ethnically, sexually, and abilitywise.

Since my first Math Solution course, I have randomly grouped the children every three weeks by having them draw playing cards. Anyone drawing an ace goes to team one; anyone drawing a two goes to team two; and so forth. Sometimes there is one girl with three boys, and sometimes two people who talk a great deal are in the same team, but we all adjust because it is only for three weeks. Many times, the children actually get to know and like someone they thought they could never tolerate. And, sometimes being the only boy in a team of girls isn't the worst situation to be in after all.

By working in groups of four on many of their learning activities, children get more opportunities to explain their thinking and get feedback on that thinking. It takes at least a month or longer at the beginning of the year to set the tone for how cooperative learning will work in my classroom. I am frequently interrupting their work for all of us to talk together, sitting on the rug in front of the room. We discuss why the groups that are working well together are able to do so and we ask groups that are having problems to explain the specifics. Then all of us make suggestions. "If Tom is taking over, speak up and let him know you are feeling left out. If you don't understand what your group is doing, ask questions."

Looking At Students

I particularly like 5th grade. The children are eager to learn and they are not too involved in the boy-girl world yet. Fifth graders have one foot firmly on the shore of childhood, but they are testing the waters of adolescence with the other foot. They can think abstractly and make leaps in understanding. They can discuss and work independently and they are full of questions. I like that.

Fifth grade is a year of contrasts. In our class, when we are immigrating from all over the world to Island Ellis Angel, 5th graders eagerly dress for the occasion and bring dolls to represent children. At the same time they sit patiently riveted during sex education discussions, and they can hardly wait to square dance each time we arrive at a fort on our westward journey on the Oregon Trail.

Discipline problems rarely occur in my classroom because there is variety and involvement of the learner throughout the day. I limit my talking to 20 minutes every hour or hour and a half. The rest of the time, the students are involved in a learning activity or coming together for a discussion. I keep my finger on the pulse of the class and on individuals in the class so I sense when it is time to change the pace of things. If the activity is too overwhelming, we meet on the rug to discuss how we can change it to fit their needs or we simply switch gears to something else. There is no sense squeezing blood out of a turnip of an activity just because it is in the lesson plan. I believe my students have a calm trust in my ability to set a comfortable stage for learning.

Class Meetings to Solve Social Problems

In the 5th grade we can also begin with class meetings to deal with social problems such as name calling or leaving children out of games on the yard. I have found that children pull together like a family when we talk closely on the rug as problems develop. There is often empathy for the person who is being called names and an open sharing of "how I felt when that happened to me." This talking through the hurt is especially important when it comes to racial name calling in classrooms such as mine with a rich mixture of ethnic backgrounds.

Also, 5th grade is a time for many talks about "being left out." Girls especially are beginning to form cliques, so it is critical that both sides have a chance to discuss openly why this is happening and what can be done about it. We talk about steps each party can take to solve the problem in a fair way. It helps to have things out on the table. Children really do care for one another and have insightful things to say.

Learning to Reason, Interpret, Understand

Most of us in the upper grades of elementary school have moved away from teaching reading as a preoccupation with phonics, workbooks, and basal readers to a curriculum based on literature. The children are reading novels with rich, not limited language. They are answering questions that require them to think through their own interpretations of the author's meaning, and then to explain these interpretations orally or in writing, using proof from the story. There are no right answers and factual questions are not the focus. Instead, the child's reasoning and understanding are given front stage. The children are honored as thinkers, not memorizers. Besides interpreting the author's meaning, the children are often asked to put themselves in the character's shoes.

In history, we use the textbook as one of several resources, not the only resource. Instead, we involve the children with primary source materials such as photographs and oral histories. We have the children relive certain time periods through simulations; they make decisions and think about approaches to problems such as how to deal with taxation without representation, or whether to take a shortcut as they approach Fort Bridger on the Oregon Trail. The children are active problem solvers and interpreters of information.

They write diary entries or letters as if they are living that moment of history, as if they are immigrating to America at the turn of the century. They are no longer just memorizing dates and events or going page by page through a textbook. Often the books the children are reading are tied to the time period they are studying.

Barriers to a Problem-Solving Curriculum in Math

There are several barriers to getting teachers unstuck from a textbook approach to mathematics. First of all, where do they turn for a whole mathematics curriculum based on problem solving and touching all the strands of number, geometry, statistics and probability, measurement, logic, pattern and function, and algebra? In the Bay Area, we are fortunate to have a number of good staff development programs in mathematics, but these groups offer a potpourri of activities from which the teacher must pick and choose as he or she tries to plan for the whole year.

It is a real challenge as we are now caught between what used to be the mathematics curriculum—the textbook—and meaningful problem-solving units. It is an exciting time, but it can be overwhelming to the teacher who also has to plan for three or four other subjects each day.

The general public provides another barrier to getting teachers unstuck from a textbook approach to mathematics. Parents, politicians, and school board members feel that they know what mathematics education should be, based on their own school experience. Most of their school experience has been teacher led, textbook oriented. The general public looks to mathematics as the subject that separates only the few best and brightest from the rest of the school population. Testing is used extensively to do this sorting.

Standardized tests create barriers to real change in the curriculum. As long as the current multiple-choice tests drive the curriculum, mathematics is not open-ended and problem solving; it is pages of algorithms in the number strand only. Fifth grade students are required to divide fractions and I assume we are to continue teaching this procedure by saying, as we were told, "Yours is not to reason why, just invert and multiply."

Albany Unified School District has encouraged and strongly supported change in the way we approach mathematics K–8. Still, the district adopted a new and harder standardized test this past year with more emphasis on the number strand. This is a double message to teachers, because textbook teaching is much more in line with these tests. Our mathematics program does not need to be confined to the standardized tests' narrow view of what mathematics should be.

If the California Assessment Program is allowed to be funded again, there will be many more open-ended items in mathematics. Our students will need to "reason why" to do well on these tests.[4]

Teachers Riding the Wave of Change

It is a complex undertaking to move teachers whose approach is rather routine and teacher-centered to a more active child-centered approach. I work as a math staff developer and as a mentor teacher in my own district. In these jobs, I share my enthusiasm for the problem-solving strategies my students are using, and I share with other teachers the stages I have gone through as a math teacher. Being a practicing classroom teacher gives me some credibility in their eyes; and the fact that my class size is large and my students are ethnically diverse gives me additional credibility. In some parts of the state or the country, the fact that I live in Berkeley, California, may cause teachers to feel my ideas are a little far out, but I am quick to point to the new National Council of Teachers of Mathematics' *Standards,* and *Everybody Counts—A Report to the Nation on the Future of Mathematics Education,* by the National Research Council. Both of these documents stress the need for mathematics teachers to move away from teaching by telling and having children memorize rules, to encouraging students' active learning and problem solving with concrete materials and continual oral and written communication of their thinking. Until textbooks change dramatically, they need to be set aside.

Teaching the Parents: New Ways to Learn

It is important that parents understand what we are doing with a literature-based curriculum instead of using basal readers and workbooks. They also need to have a feeling for what the writing process involves when children are readers of their own work and choosers of their own topics. In math, parents need to feel secure that changes are meaningful—a move away from a focus on number and pages of algorithms toward more collaborative problem solving in geometry, probability and statistics, logic, and measurement. Parents' own schooling involved basal readers, books with grammar, punctuation, and capitalization rules, and math textbooks with pages of exercises, so naturally changes make them a little unsure.

On Back to School Night in September, I share my philosophy and try to involve the parents in some activities which give them a feel for what we do in my room. Just before Parent Teacher Conferences in November and again in March, my classroom has a FAMILY MATH[5] and Computer Evening when the children are the teachers and have their parents do some of the math problem-solving activities with concrete materials and educational software the children have used. Then, when we have our conference, the parents have a feeling for what the math program involves; they feel reassured and are often excited about math.

Parents are very supportive when they understand what you are doing and why you are doing it. I do appreciate it when I get parent support on field trips three or four times each year, at our FAMILY MATH and Computer Evenings twice a year, and on our two Play Evenings each year. It does a lot for the children to share their understanding in math and their emotions in drama with their families. These are proud moments for 5th grade learners.

Working It Out With Each Child

I keep parents informed about the curriculum and the child's performance, but in this fifth year I do ask at Back to School Night that the parents begin to back out of the picture more and more. I continue to send home monthly newsletters and I type up a lengthy weekly homework list with meaningful activities in every subject, but I rarely call parents.

My line with the students is, "You are in the 5th grade now and the ball is in your court as a learner. You can do it. If you are confused, call me at home or come before school for study hall." I put so much of my time into curriculum and into relating to the children during the school day that I save my evenings for my own family.

Many students come from difficult home situations. There are a few who are in joint custody where they split their time between two households each week. Others are alone for dinner and homework each evening. Some children get themselves and their siblings up, fed, and off to school each morning with no adult help. During parent-teacher conferences in my first few years in Albany and in my last year at Richmond, most parents were so overwhelmed with their own lives and their own jobs or marital situations, that dealing with their child's school work or behavior was more than they could handle.

Whether it's behavior or an academic issue, I find it most successful to deal directly with the child and not to involve the parent. I've accommodated; sometimes I come as early as 7 to get my planning done so I can run a study hall from 8 to 8:30 for the children who need extra help or need to talk privately. I also eat lunch with a small group of children each week.

By the time the children are 10 or 11, we can begin to deal with home problems at this level: "I really feel for you. I know what happened at home last night. I know your mom got drunk and then tried to pick you up. When you refused to go with her, she ran away. I understand why you are acting out today. Let's just take some time out. Why don't you go and work on the computer for a while, do what you want for an hour, and then let's go on with what we have to do today." I don't call the parents. Instead the child and I find a workable solution here in the classroom.

I rarely involve the family unless I think a child is being abused at home or I am failing to make headway with the child academically or emotionally. Then I also intervene with the proper people. We have a superb support staff of school psychologist, speech and language therapist, reading resource teacher, and resource specialist. Also the on-site principal is very helpful. At times like this, you need to hear other people's thinking and sometimes call for a problem-solving session with the parent. When there is a terrible conflict between the parents in a divorce situation and the child is just being ripped apart, I've even gone so far as to get the assistant superintendent involved. The child has to have an advocate.

Student Teachers and Collaborative Teaching

In Albany, we are asked to take student teachers, and I have done so the last three years. For many years I refused because we receive no compensation for this task and we are given no special privileges at Cal [University of California at Berkeley]. I felt that public school teachers are too often asked to go the extra mile, so I refused to take on the added responsibility of a student teacher. Then I began to soften as I saw the high quality of student teachers we were getting and I realized I could limit myself to only those students who already had three semesters of classroom experience through the Developmental Teacher Education Master's Program.

I have now had three student teachers and the experience has been energizing. These teachers are interested in curriculum, well informed about children's developmental stages, and work in a caring way with the students. Having another person to teach with is an optimum experience; you can bounce ideas off one another in the heat of the action and share reflections on individual children, then jointly decide what the next step should be. Just as collaborative learning gives children opportunities to learn from one another, collaborative teaching has the same benefits.

Also, I find much of what I do in teaching is rather instinctual and my student teachers ask questions that force me to clarify my thinking on what I'm doing and why. Their questions really force me to be clear on my purpose—Why don't I give class points? Why do I allow children to write so many rough drafts without asking them to take more pieces to final draft?

As I observe my student teachers taking over the classroom, I am struck by the developmental stages in a teacher's learning. So often, new teachers try to cover too much territory in a lesson and rush on to finish without hearing the children or readjusting the pace or the focus to the students' needs. Also, new teachers tend to talk too much and try to pour in too much information, instead of listening and drawing more from the children's thoughts. I share my thinking when I can, but I often wonder if it is a stage we all must go through before we really understand what we are doing.

In a classroom that values children's thoughts in every subject area and requires the teacher to make educational decisions for the next day's activities based on those thoughts, it helps having two of us listening. Always, we need to urge each other to do less content and allow more time for children to clarify the "what and why" of their own thinking.

What Colleagues Offer Each Other

There are pressures in teaching in Albany. Its reputation means a great deal. When I first arrived, board members seemed to be in the schools often and the central administration was right down the hall. Although we rarely saw the administrators, I overreacted by focusing on impressive activities and covering too much content. I wanted to prove that I too could be a "great teacher" like my next-door colleague and I overdid it. I was thinking more of myself and what other people were thinking of me and I wasn't listening to the children. I wasn't feeling the pulse of the class. That first year was a disaster.

I also wasn't opening up to my colleagues and that was a big mistake. Now I have taught eight years in Albany and the teachers at my school are the reason I stay. They are very informed professionals who are always discussing curriculum and children and learning. There is a real support system here. When things are happening in one's personal life, people jump right in. They care deeply.

There is also a deep commitment to the job. This commitment results in the Albany Schools' strong reputation. The staff puts in a lot of time and I appreciate that. Because I work fairly hard at my job, I would resent it if people were on site only from 8:30 to 3:30. After school, I like meeting in a teacher's classroom to talk about educational issues, site events, and children. It is a good feeling when I come in on the weekends and am able to toss ideas about and share materials with my colleagues who are here too. I am never alone.

We are also a staff who enjoys one another's company. Several of us were in a book discussion group together with our significant others for a couple of years. Some of the faculty met regularly in a writing group and several of us did Jane Fonda workout tapes two or three days a week after school in my classroom for an entire year.

Hazards of Top-Down Management

Our faculty is also a group that takes strong—very strong—stands, and I appreciate that. Unfortunately, even in small districts, the model is top-down management. Often decisions have a negative impact on us; the people at the top are far from the classroom. This top-down model means that teachers are evaluated every other year by the principal and this is often the only time principals come into the classroom when the children are there. Principals, however, are not evaluated by teachers.

One year, an administrator sent a list to those of us who needed to be evaluated. He wanted us to think of four or five areas we planned to grow in and to outline the goals for ourselves in each of these areas. I was feeling, "I just can't stretch that much. I am trying so hard and this request is overwhelming. How can I possibly grow in depth in five areas of my teaching all in one year?" It turns out several of us felt this was asking too much so the union representative for our school talked to the principal and he made a more realistic request.

There is too much of a gap in education between the policymakers, the administration, and the people in the trenches, the teachers. Often, administrators have had very little teaching experience.

I for one would like to see the situation where the principalship would be rotated among the teachers. In that way, the teachers would get a feeling for the difficulties of being an administrator and the principal would never be more than a year or two away from being in the classroom again. The principal would be much more aware of what has to happen to support a classroom where the children are learning in a meaningful, exciting way and the teacher is feeling fulfilled, not overwhelmed.

Salaries and Working Hours

In the fall of 1988, the entire staff met almost weekly for three months to discuss ways to pressure the administration into giving us a decent salary increase. (I'll say more about this later.) We were completely united and all of us worked very hard before and after school hours picketing, writing position papers, and leafleting. It was a proud moment when we succeeded in raising the salary schedule, but it took enormous strength of purpose with each of us pitching in.

Many of the teachers here have taught 20 to 25 years. Their salaries have not kept up with inflation, so they have been losing money yearly. The public, even though they support the schools, expect us to do more with fewer supplies, with more children in the classroom, and with less salary.

The public says we have an 8:30–3:30 day. I myself put in 10–12 hours a school day and at least five to ten hours on the weekends. Most teachers I'm associated with are this dedicated. In elementary school, for every hour we teach, it takes at least an additional hour for preparation and follow-through. Although we work a 9 and 1/2 month school year, if you were to divide out the hours into 40-hour weeks, we are working all but a few weeks each year.

I like feeling on top of things. I like feeling I'm doing a good job, but when I'm always getting the message, "Now we're asking you to do this, and we expect this and that," pretty soon it gets to be overwhelming. It becomes too stressful. You never feel you are doing enough and then you become less enthusiastic about your work. You become burned out. I feel for the teachers in many districts who have been working without any real support financially or supplywise, and in difficult situations. It's hard to say "No" even to excessive demands, because we are public employees.

Five Years of Layoff Notices in Richmond

In 1981 I had decided I wanted to be with a classroom of children full time, instead of working as a resource teacher. I missed bonding with individual children over a long period of time. Also, my own children were getting older and it helped us financially to have me working full time. I took a 3rd-4th combination class in San Pablo, which is part of the Richmond Unified School District. That was a toughie, a really tough job. I'd say the whole class was needy, emotionally, economically, and academically, tremendously needy. I worked so hard that year.

I was highly thought of in Richmond where I had worked as a resource teacher since 1974. I did several all-district staff development sessions on writing, but no matter how much they thought of me, I had to be laid off every year on March 15th. After five straight years, it began to wear on my feelings of self worth as a teacher. I was so angry after the fifth layoff year, I decided to take unemployment payments that summer, although I hadn't done that before. I took the money and wallpapered a couple of rooms in our house. It was my way of getting back at the system.

After being back in the classroom full time in 1981–1982, the man in personnel said he would let me know where, not if, there would be openings. I was assured that there would be a place for me in the fall either as a resource teacher or as a classroom teacher, and they asked me to check in on August 16th. I remember that. I drove to the district office and things had changed dramatically over the summer. Not only were there no openings full time, but there were no openings for resource teachers. They asked me to wait until the day school started again.

A Job in Albany, and 80 Applicants

I'm the kind of person who has a certain amount of pride. I was angry and I was frustrated because I do work very hard at my profession. To feel like a number that just gets tossed around when you put out so much energy was getting to me. In August 1982, I took the freeway off-ramp to come up Solano Avenue because I had errands to do, and thought, "I'm going to stop at Albany Unified and see if they have any openings." They had a 5th grade opening, and the closing for this application was within two days. I took the application form in a rather defiant mood and decided, "I'm going to go for it."

I got my principal from the previous year—who would have given anything to have me back in his school but his hands were tied—and the principal at a school where I had been a resource teacher, to write me recommendations. I spent a couple of days filling out a résumé; I hadn't done that since the mid-60s. I had gotten my Master's degree, but I hadn't set up a professional folder. There were around 80 applicants for this one position. They narrowed it down by paper screening to—I don't know, maybe five or seven people—and then four people were interviewed. Then that was further narrowed down to three; each of the three had an interview with the superintendent, and I got the job. I had to get ready to teach within a week and a half.

Tenure, March 15, and Layoff in Albany

When I began teaching in Albany you did not get tenure until the first day of your fourth year of teaching. In 1986, I finally got tenure and felt I had some job security at long last, but I received a layoff notice on March 15 of that year because the district was very tight on funds.

Legally, the district has to let teachers know by March 15 if there is a possibility of layoff. They did that to a large number of people, I think it was 42 out of a district faculty of 150. At this school there were ten of us who received layoff notices, and it was really hard because it hadn't happened in Albany before. Many of us were taken completely by surprise. I certainly was.

All school districts in California give notices on March 15 and then you are to teach until the end of the year, another three months away. It's hoped that you will teach with the same enthusiasm and energy and forward-looking attitude as in the past, but the notice takes something out of you, especially if you are a single parent providing for a family on a very tight income. These teachers have to think ahead in terms of, "Where else can I apply? Where am I going to scramble to get a job?" I wasn't in that position. My husband was working and I wasn't the full provider, but emotionally and professionally, it takes something out of you to know that you're just going to be blanket laid off.[6]

The Process of Hearings

The experience of being laid off was even worse for us because of a process that provides for hearings. Albany Unified did follow that process, so all of us who were laid off had to go through two days of hearings. Very little information was given to us about what was going to happen during this hearing, but substitutes were hired for all of us.

The superintendent and his attorney gave their side and told why there was limited money and why they had to send lay-off notices. Then each of us was given an opportunity to go up on a stage. I suppose we were the accused. There was an administrative law judge and there was a lawyer for us, a lawyer who came through the union. He was very little help to us and really wasn't able to answer any of our questions. It was sort of a vacuum; we didn't know what was expected of us.

The first day they started calling teachers in the afternoon to the witness stand, and the administrative law judge let them explain what their teaching experience had been and why they felt they should be rehired. Each teacher was able to bare his or her soul a little which I thought was very therapeutic for those of us who were listening. It helped us feel like valued individuals with faces and feelings, not replaceable parts. We were called in alphabetical order, and I wasn't called until the afternoon of the second day. As usual, I was eager to speak.

Devaluing What Happens in the Classroom

By that time, the lawyer for the administration was getting a little tired of hearing us explain from our hearts why we were good teachers. At lunchtime, she met with the judge. I was the first person to speak after lunch. The judge asked me the same questions, "What have you done with the district, and why do you think they should rehire you?"

I started talking about the things I had done for the district such as School Site Council and the holistic scoring of writing, then I said, "But the most important thing is what happens in my classroom." At that point the lawyer for the district said, "Objection, Your Honor, this is irrelevant information," and His Honor said, "Objection sustained." I was the first teacher who was cut off and I had to step down at that point. The people after me were also cut off. It was not that I was being pinpointed, it was just that the day was getting long and they were tired of hearing our heart-felt messages.

To me that ruling was symbolic of what takes place too often in education: what happens in my classroom is not what is important. What I can do that gets public attention is important. It's not the little things that happen on a day-to-day basis in the classroom between children and the teacher that count. It's what the district can say about us in a newsletter.

Teachers' Salaries and Professional Options

Salaries for beginning teachers have risen dramatically across California. When I first came to Albany in 1982, a beginning teacher with just an AB made $12,000; in 1988 that teacher made $21,000. However, a teacher who has taught 13 years or more suffers from two constraints. First, the salary levels off and second, if she wishes to change districts she is penalized. Whenever a superintendent moves to another district, *his* salary goes up. Whenever a teacher moves to another district, *her* salary goes back to Step 5. She may have taught 25 years, but she is paid as if she has only five years' experience.

The monetary rewards go to those who leave their teaching careers behind and go into administration. This is wrong. Top teachers should be kept in the classroom and they should be paid accordingly. In Albany, the superintendent's salary has risen significantly in eight years. To get decent pay raises, teachers must go through painful public battles. The salaries of administrators are raised quietly.

Obviously I do not stay in teaching for the money. I stay because of the aliveness of the profession, but these questions concern me deeply: If it is going to be this way, if the money is always going to be tight, if the demands are always going to be increasing, how can I keep up the pace long enough for a decent retirement?

Lottery, Proposition 13, and Public Responsibilities

I was a history major in college, and grew up in a household of fairly liberal Democrats, people who believe strongly in public education. I believe in it too. I find the idea—that we have come to the point where the California lottery is supposed to be the answer for our financial woes and that public education is going to be bailed out by gambling—absolutely unacceptable.[7] I think it is abrogating the responsibility that we as a state, that we as a nation, should have to provide the support that keeps us strong. The whole core of our country has been its belief in public education. We have, at least in this state, a tremendous number of immigrant families from other countries, and I think public education is a must.

The amount of money California funds per pupil for public education is inadequate. I think Prop. 13 was wrong, but inadequate funding is happening nationally too. Funding education or funding health or funding housing or funding humanities is not a high priority. Funding Savings and Loan bailouts is more important. I don't see these priorities changing even though George Bush is supposed to be the education president.

California has a very high pupil-teacher ratio—30 to 1. There's a lot of talk out there, but not much action is being taken to remedy the situation. Presently the K–5 enrollment in Albany is the highest it has been since I began teaching here eight years ago.

The school administration has a responsibility to promote learning and to provide it for the district's children. These children do not get a second opportunity to visit 5th grade—this is it. The administration and the board set the priorities for the district and K–5 class size must be attended to. It would help if the site administrator and the central administrators would spend time in classrooms getting a feel for the the way class size impacts the type of education that we are attempting and they are encouraging.

Process-Intensive Teaching vs. Ballooning Class Size

The classrooms are overly crowded. Still, we teachers continue to try a process approach to learning where children's interpretive thoughts are honored in literature, where the children listen to and respond to one another's writing, and where children's own strategies in solving math problems are valued. When the adult-pupil ratio is 1 to 30 in a 5th grade classroom, this kind of interactive teaching becomes overwhelming. The individual children do not get the attention they need and the teacher is stretched to the breaking point. In this situation it is much easier to pull out the textbook and have each child work quietly filling in blanks.

The district pays overage money to those of us who have one or two children over the contractual limit. This money must be spent on classroom supplies or aide time. We get $9.53 a day for four days, not the five days in a school week. This amounts to less pay than a babysitter makes.

The administration seems to feel that class size is a contractual, not an educational, issue. It is true that many districts are creeping up to the 60s class size of around 35 children in a classroom. Many of us taught then and we used textbooks, workbooks, and pages of fill-in-the-blanks worksheets. The kind of thinking and discussing, not just memorizing and regurgitating, curriculum we are trying in our classrooms today cannot survive with the 60s class size.

Benefits of Teaching Teachers

The past couple of years, I have been privileged to work once a month as a math staff developer for the California Math Leadership Program in Oakland and I have traveled around the country doing The Math Solution workshops for Marilyn Burns. Also, I am one of twenty 5th grade teachers in California who will be running staff development sessions for 1,500 5th grade teachers on the "Seeing Fractions" unit. The unit was developed by the Used Number Project as a 4-to-6 unit that teachers may use to replace their textbook teaching of fractions.

Here I am, almost 50 years old, at the midpoint in my career, and some people think I do have something to offer in helping teachers rethink their approach to education. I am even being paid as if I were someone with some expertise. I never dreamed I'd have this opportunity to work with such a fine group of educators who, like myself, are constantly refining their thinking on how children learn and stretching professionally as they plan workshops nightly with one another and as they talk with the participants the next day.

These are rare moments for me, and all this meaningful work helps me return to the classroom with a renewed belief about the importance of what happens there and an eagerness to try once again. I wish more career teachers had these opportunities at this stage in their teaching.

As I speak in this book or during staff development sessions, there is an added benefit. I am forced to articulate my views about education and the reasons for these views. My beliefs certainly change in subtle ways as I continue to grow as a teacher, but until I can clearly explain my thinking about how children learn through active involvement with their minds in all subject areas, how can I influence the public, the politicians, and the administrators in my own district?

Students as Self-Confident Learners

When I think of my students, I feel I have done my job if the children come out of my classroom believing in themselves as learners. I hope that my students feel confident that they can read their own writing critically and make appropriate revisions. I hope they can make sense out of rich mathematical problems and can explain or diagram their own understanding of the problems. I hope they can read literature and go beneath what an author says to what an author means and connect that meaning to their own lives.

I feel I do encourage my students to be independent learners who are willing to take risks. They are people who don't always have to have the quick right answer, so they are willing to be persistent as they construct their own understanding and come up with their own wonderful ideas.

I am not a touchy-feely kind of person. I would like to be, and I am getting so I am more demonstrative. I find myself hugging kids more now and I think that's very good for them and for me. It's a communication of closeness and I'm liking that, but it has taken some work on my part. In my staff development work, I am finding that adults welcome openness and warmth too, so I am trying to share more of my inner self now.

Magic and Action

With all the problems, I really do enjoy teaching, and I think that is what keeps most of us in the profession. It certainly isn't the money or the public acclaim. There is something magical about working with children, hearing their ideas, seeing them explain and diagram their thinking, and feeling their excitement about learning.

Teaching is a fascinating, creative, warm profession, with a lot of action. As a middle-aged person, having all that action and involvement is very meaningful to me. I feel young inside. I feel enthusiastic, and I feel creative in my profession. I like that.

Elois Irvin:
A Love of Math and Regard for Colleagues

Wanting to be Like the Teacher

My mother had an old bell with a clapper in it; when we would play school, I would always get to be the teacher. I had six brothers and just one sister but we girls were sort of domineering when it came to overpowering the boys.

I had some good early experiences with teachers, particularly my 4th, 5th, and 6th grade teacher, and I probably was influenced by her more than anybody else. She was a dainty kind of person, very firm, competent, and attentive to students, and she took an early interest in me. She would visit my home, my parents, and take me home with her on the weekend. She had a daughter who was a lot older than I, and I guess I was a little playmate for her, kind of like her doll. I would do things at her house that I didn't do at mine. I remember the first time that I ever ate goose liver, for example, and I thought that was kind of funny. She had a piano and I always loved to play piano. I liked everything about her, and I wanted to be like her.

Developing Confidence in Math

I grew up in Montgomery, Alabama, and went to school there. It was a rural part of the county, a very slow-moving part of the world. I have several relatives who are teachers, including my mother and two aunts. I was in Atlanta from the 8th grade through college.

I went to an all-Black high school; the staff and faculty were all Black and very competent. My role model was my high school geometry teacher who did not spend a whole lot of time lecturing. I must have felt that was a better way to teach. He had us working together, working at the board, working in a group over here and over there. He'd leave us alone.

He always had a lot of energy. He was a little short man; he'd run in the door and say, "I'm ready. Are you ready? If you aren't ready, you should have stayed home today." That was the way he was. You couldn't just sit there and not do anything. He'd say, "You can't sit there next year. We need the seat. You've got to do something, you've got to get out of here."

When I went to college, there were several of us who majored in mathematics, and I'm sure that my math teacher had a lot of influence on us. I had developed confidence that I could do math, and so I just jumped right in. As the years progressed, there were always more men in my classes, and most of the teachers were men, but again, I had a lot of support there. I met some really serious students and we learned to study together. We'd find a little room someplace and go in and work problems. I did very well in college, I liked it.

Teaching as a Math Major

When I first went to college—to Morris Brown, which is one of the United Negro College Fund schools, more than 100 years old—I thought I still wanted to be a teacher but I was sort of torn between majoring in math or English. I pursued the math major and wound up with about enough units to minor in English. Of course, back then there were not a lot of options as far as professions were concerned if you were Black. For example, I never saw a real computer until I came to California, when I was 25 years old. I had never touched a computer before then and I had majored in mathematics.

The only career that I ever thought about was teaching, but I did think about whether to teach after graduation or go to graduate school. I ended up going into teaching in 1959 because there was a great demand for teachers. At that time, we didn't have much money. I lived with my grandmother and I felt that she had made so many sacrifices for me, I thought I'd just go to work. In the summers, I went to Atlanta University where you could take good strong math courses and earn a Master's degree.

My first job was teaching high school math in a little town called Cairo in southeast Georgia. I picked that job because the principal of the school seemed to have such a dire need. He wouldn't let go. He'd call about every other week, "Have you decided?" I started right after graduation, and I didn't have a teaching credential because I had chosen the math major instead of the math education major. He said, "We don't care whether you have a certificate or not."

It turned out to be a wonderful experience for me, and maybe for the students too. I was very young and I went to a new part of the state; I had never even been to that part of the world. It was a small town, mostly a rural area, but the kids were from a lot of different areas surrounding the town. My first students were 11th and 12th graders and I felt real comradeship with them because I wasn't much older than they were.

A Party and Nice Behavior

In Georgia, the kids were very poor. I look at people here in California who are on welfare and who say that they are poor and I think, "They don't know what being poor is like. Those were kids who never got enough to eat, who never had decent clothes to wear."

For Christmas I said, "Are we going to have a party?" Having a party implies there will be some nice behavior and some nice things going on. My grandmother said, "Yes, have a party. Feed them." She had the butcher cut a ham for her and she baked it for me and brought this round bread—I remember, they had never seen round bread before—and she made potato salad. Here I go on that morning before Christmas vacation starts with all this stuff, and we had a banquet. I learned so much from them. I learned a lot about their attitudes.

The Big Time and Two Worlds

After a year in Cairo and two years teaching in Athens, I was ready for the big time. By then I had gotten my credential and I had accepted a position at a large high school in Atlanta, not the one that I had attended, but one on the other side of town. It was a very urban, very poor area with typical urban problems.

I had gone to the largest high school in Atlanta and enjoyed my experiences there, but there were definitely two different worlds in that one school. I remembered what the other world looked like, and I wasn't quite sure that I would be able to handle all the problems I knew came with it.

I accepted the job and found a supportive staff; that makes all the difference in the world. If I had felt that I was out there all by myself and had to figure out everything by myself, I don't think I would have stayed there more than a year. Atlanta was good, a very good experience. The faculty was large, but within our department it was small enough for gatherings, usually at lunchtime, sometimes after school, just sitting and talking.

There were opportunities to go to school in the summer and I felt I needed to update myself. I took a math class through a National Science Foundation math project at Atlanta University, and the teaching staff was just excellent. I never met a professor that I liked more than the one I had that summer teaching foundations of math. He was able to communicate very simply. His philosophy was, "If you search diligently enough, you can find a rather simple way to explain most things." When I went back to teaching in my own school, my program reflected his style.

Systems Engineering vs. The Satisfactions of Teaching

In 1966 I decided to get married. My husband had been in the Navy here at Treasure Island, and he thought that California was the place to live, so that's how I got here. I had to resign my teaching position, and I thought, "Maybe this is a chance to consider something other than teaching. Gee, working for IBM sounds like a glamorous job, I think I'll try it."

I was hired as a systems engineer even though I had never touched a computer. In six weeks I had to learn everything about their computers, including five different computer languages and enough to go out in the field with the other members of the team. It was demanding. Our accounts were people in education, but it wasn't a very enjoyable experience for me. The most exciting thing that I did was write a program to score teacher-made tests.

It did not have the same feeling of satisfaction as teaching, and I found after the first year that I really wished that I was teaching again. The money at IBM was a little better than teaching, and the opportunity for growth was there. You could go on and earn a lot of money, but it wasn't enough to make me say, "I'll do this even if I don't like it." In fact, I haven't found a job yet that makes me do that.

After two years with IBM, there was a demand for math teachers, in 1968–69. Michael, my second child, was just born. I went to Richmond Unified School District and applied; in a day or two, I had the job.* It was almost September and time for school to start. I was a little bit wary of teaching junior high because I hadn't done that, but I knew that I preferred teaching to doing anything else.

---

*In October 1990, the Richmond Unified School District enrolled 31,575 students and employed approximately 1,600 teachers. In its 37 elementary schools, the student population was: 34.2% African American; 12.2% Asian/Pacific Islanders; 4.9% Filipino; 17% Hispanic; .4% Native American; and 30.9% White. In the district's 11 middle schools and high schools, the student population was: 36.1% African American; 12.7% Asian/Pacific Islanders; 5.8% Filipino; 13.8% Hispanic; .3% Native American; and 31% White. In Richmond Unified, the percentage of families on AFDC is compiled by school; at Kennedy High School, where Elois Irvin teaches, 41% of the students' families receive AFDC.

Hog Heaven in a Math Program

After teaching in junior high school, there were some surprises when I went back to a high school position. The first one had to do with the teaching assignment. The vice principal who was in charge of the school program was aware that I had a minor in English, and the best program that they offered me was a combination of math and English. I felt unsuited for the task, and I was unwilling to be in a position where I didn't feel that I knew what I was doing. I stayed with it for that year, but I told her at the end of the year that if there wasn't a math position for me at Kennedy I wanted to be transferred to a school where there was one. My colleagues in math heard about this and said, "Oh no, you can't leave."

They prevailed upon her to find or create a math position for me and so I stayed. I was serious, though. I would not have accepted a combination like that. I like English but I did not feel comfortable teaching it. I felt that the teachers in the department had their own specialties and only taught what they liked to teach: you had the teacher who liked drama, who spent a lot of time on drama; you had the teacher who taught grammar who never asked the students to write an essay. And so I was assigned a math program for the next year in Kennedy. It's been like being in hog heaven.

Teachers' Role and Parents' Attitudes

When I was teaching in Georgia, a teacher complained to a parent, I don't remember what about. The parent came to the school and whipped the child in front of the class; devastated the teacher. She said after that she was never going to call another parent. The parent felt that that was what he was supposed to do; well, at least he felt that he was supposed to correct that particular situation. I don't want that, but I do want parental support, and I think that a lot of times it isn't there.

Parents have so many problems with their children themselves; they are not in control. A lot of times the school is the only place that the child goes where he's perfectly satisfied to be. I have seen parents come to the school, and I'm embarrassed at the way the child treats the parent. That is a really sad situation. I think it has a lot to do with expectation.

That's one of the reasons I like to know my students and I like to know their parents, because I want their parents to know me as a person, and to know me as a teacher, and to know that I am the teacher. I know what I'm supposed to do, and I'm doing what I'm supposed to do. My feeling is,

"While I will listen to you, I'm not going to let you tell me how to do my job. I'm going to do my job because I know how to do it."

Children today bring with them a lot more problems from home. They've got other concerns that get in the way. If children way back then had gone to school without food, I think the teacher would have gone to the home. Teachers always visited the homes of their children and they had a better feel for what the family life was like. It wasn't considered prying; it was part of the job.

There was a confidence among the public that teachers knew what to teach, and how to teach. It was not the public's job to tell them what to teach and how to teach it; the teachers were going to do it and the parents were going to support them.

Adults don't see the problems first-hand that the students do: the drug scene, for example. You know it's there but it's not always right in front of you. The teacher has to recognize that the job does not end with teaching subject matter, that subject matter is probably the last thing you teach. You know, there's the question about whether or not the teacher teaches morals. I say, "What a silly question. Of course you teach morals, either directly or indirectly and sometimes both." I have had kids I've told, "That was mean," and their behavior was mean; and there's no other way to describe it.

I tell them, "When you leave school, other teachers do not have to take you home with them. They can go to the suburbs and forget about you. You'll see me. I'll be in the grocery store, and I'll wave at you, especially if you're with a parent. I may go over and introduce myself if you don't hurry up and introduce me to your parents." That's the way I want to be known: "This lady doesn't act like a teacher. She's just like everybody else."

Except, "You must be respectful and I'm not going to have it any other way. And yes, we all have bad days. Nobody is hopeless. If you were, you wouldn't keep coming every day." That's really what I tell other teachers. If the kids didn't expect something to happen, they wouldn't come to school, especially high school kids because they can find a whole lot of other things to do. Some of their parents would never know that they didn't come. But I find the kids to be very open and honest, and they conform to what I expect of them, usually.

Willing to Change, Willing to Borrow Ideas

I have never worked in a school where math teachers were selfish. I have colleagues who are the greatest people in the world. I could not have gotten this far without their support. We teach all the college prep courses as a team. We don't want it any other way. We used to do team teaching, but we've grown so that there isn't even space now to combine two classes. My room used to be the big class where we could combine two or three classes. One person could deliver instruction to an advanced algebra group, say two days a week. The content of it could be generalized in such a way that the rest of the time in small groups you could get to work with the students in a closer setting. We don't have that any more, but we still plan together. We still discuss philosophy.

Right now we're going through the calculator thing. How much should students use calculators and where? Some people have to be convinced, you know. I think one of the best ways to do that is by example. A lot of times teachers might be willing to try things but they aren't sure it's going to work for them. Sometimes if you just do it, or do it with somebody else, you feel better about doing it.

I've seen us change a lot, I've seen us change the way we teach a lot of things. There is reassurance, for example, that there's nothing lost when the students use calculators versus using the tables and all these long-drawn-out calculations, interpolating, and all that stuff. I think it's important for students to know what it means and even to see it done, but I don't think they necessarily need to know how to do that.

I think no matter how old I get I'll be willing to try new things. I'm willing to change the way I do things if I think there's something better. I'm willing to share and borrow from the other guy too. Sometimes that helps a lot. Sometimes a teacher has an idea and I can say, "Yes, let me try your idea too."

Who Sets Rules?

The faculty doesn't ignore the problems of student conflicts either. They don't pretend that the problems don't exist. If the teachers are very competent, they can be assertive. We tell our students, not only did they get a teacher, they got a mother also. Probably we have more women in our math department than most school districts. In fact there are just two men; we think we should have more. But you know, we just have to say to the kids, "We don't do that in here," and they know what we're talking about. Every now and then there's a challenge, but never anything that we haven't been able to deal with. Teacher just doesn't back down.

Kids are kids and if you treat them like anything else you don't get the response that you want. They are not adults. Sometimes you can give them more responsibility than they can handle. I learned that you set goals, you don't make a lot of rules. You make them as you go if you need them. Even the kids know when you need a new rule; then you can let them make it. If they make the rules, believe me they are going to enforce them. They are stricter than the teacher is.

A number of things have gone on in the high school here in Richmond that have been positive, especially lately. We have had something called conflict management. This was an effort to teach kids how to resolve their difficulties without getting into fights and getting into real trouble with the school administration. The participants have come from all sections. They've been the high achievers, the low achievers, the kid who got suspended five times, you know, the kid who never gets in trouble, the middle of the road.

What they do is take their issues to the other students, and if there's any hint of a problem, they jump on it first. They call the students in, they sit around and talk about the problem. It's a student-run program. One of the vice principals brought the idea and he tried it, and now other schools in the district are also doing it. This summer some of those kids made presentations at an elementary school, so I think some of that philosophy is trickling on down.

How the Kids Get Along

Usually the kids themselves get along very well in this racially diverse school. Back in the 60s, when the schools were trying to balance their enrollments ethnically, Kennedy High always had a different kind of situation. It had a large number of Black students, and a fairly large percentage of Asian students; it also had a mix of middle and upper class students. There was just something about that group, they did not intimidate each other. I think that was it. White kids who are very secure have nothing to fear from Black kids, and don't fear them. Over the years it has not changed a lot.

I think most of the White kids who are still here come from middle and upper class backgrounds. It may be that is why the kids get along better; they come from secure parents. I think parents tend to be more fearful than the kids, and I'm sure that has a lot to do with it. We were talking about kids who get battered in school, and how the students decide which one will get picked on. The little White kid who goes with his head down and looks afraid, that's the one they pick on. You soar down the hall like you own the world, and they aren't interested in messing with you.

Defending the Calculus Class

We said to the district that, because they drew boundaries a certain way, there are kids who don't want to come to our school because it's in the heart of the city. Their fears are understandable; they are not always reasonable but they are understandable. The kids want to go to the school that's on the city's outskirts rather than ours, and so they find ways to get around the attendance boundaries.

One year they allowed 30 kids in the college prep classes to transfer to the other school. We teachers told them in no uncertain terms, "There is a natural attrition rate. When those kids at our school get to be seniors, if there are only 12 of them left, we are going to have a calculus class." We were going to insist that there be a calculus class, and they agreed with us, but they had already allowed the kids to transfer. There was a big stink about it then, but they couldn't go back and rescind the transfers.

Assertiveness and Geometry

Looking over my class this last year, I don't think I had a single Black male who was outstanding, even good in geometry. I had about four Black girls who were really top-notch. I think that Black males are not encouraged in this area, because in my class they were the older students and were late getting started on our college prep program. I don't think that they are encouraged.

The girls are a lot more assertive. Two of them would have been offended, I'm sure, if the teacher had said, "I don't recommend you for college prep." I mean they would have raised the roof. I don't think any of those guys would have done that, I really don't. We need to look further into this, particularly at junior high math.

Students Teach the Chairman

I am department chairman now, but I was not initially. The chairman was a man who had been teaching for maybe 30 years. I don't know how to describe him, except that I saw a lot of positive changes in him. He was one of these smart people who liked to teach only the brightest students, and the students in his class knew that. They knew that he didn't have time for you if you didn't like the fun things, and the tricky things, if you didn't catch on.

They felt that way. I don't think he was actually that way at all, I just think that was the impression he gave them.

One of the changes that I saw was the increase in the numbers of Black students who took college prep courses; you didn't have that many to start with. They were always the smartest ones. The chairman may have been a little apprehensive about working with some of those students. If you're not very secure, you may create this impression of disinterest. Teachers have feelings and apprehensions just like everybody else and, if they've not had interaction with certain types of students, they don't know how to do it.

At that time we had modular scheduling so kids could just drop in to the math office. There were kids who would come in, not necessarily Black kids, other kids too, especially girls. They would come to see him and he would say, "I'm busy right now." Sometimes as department chairman you have to write reports and stuff and he would send them away. I would say, "I'm not doing anything, I'll help you," and they'd come over.

Then I saw him stopping what he was doing and taking on students. I saw him do more and more of that. By the time he retired I think a lot more of the kids really did like him, and I think he liked more of them. He seemed a lot more relaxed. He was a smoker and they would try to get him to put his cigarettes out, and talk to him about it. Every now and again there was one who had nerve enough to crush his cigarettes, all in good nature.

For Student Teachers: Tact and Analysis

I had my first experience with supervising a student teacher in Georgia. There was no preparation for it, and maybe that's good. The student teachers came from the state college system. They had at least one or two coordinators who came and helped us get ready. My principal asked me to do it, I think it was the second year that I was there, and I felt, "Maybe there's something that he likes that's going on here."

It was a good experience. Even with the more recent student teachers I've had, I think that I've approached the work the same way. I've felt that the class is really mine and I'm responsible for whatever goes on. There was a lot of discussion with the student teachers and planning with their supervisor. It was very clear to me that my role was not telling the teacher what he should do specifically, but giving him room to try out some things and yet at the same time to have a handle on what was going on. It made me more reflective of my own teaching, and I think it still does.

If I didn't encounter a student teacher every now and then I think I would forget how really hard it is to get things in place. It doesn't just happen. You have to work at it, you have to fail sometimes, you have to try something and see that it doesn't work. We certainly had those kinds of experiences. But working tactfully and professionally with a person, I saw my role as not always giving advice but analyzing the situation, going over what happened, what might have happened if something else had been done. Even now I never say, "Do this" except "You do have some material that you have to cover."

Jerry, Who Changed Children's Lives

We had a student teacher this past year; it brings tears to my eyes. He's new to teaching. He's not a young man; he had served long enough with the military to retire, so I guess that's at least twenty years. He has young ideas and he's exuberant, and he sees teaching as a desirable profession. He has lots of other options.

He came to do student teaching, but we had a teacher who took a medical leave of absence at the end of the first quarter, so he was hired as an intern to replace her. He took over her classes, really difficult classes. She had one advanced algebra class, and she had general and practical math classes. I don't know why the kids were in such disarray. They were unmanageable. You would have had to see it to believe it, which is probably why she left. Anyway, Jerry came in and he said, "OK, I'll do this."

Jerry knew that he had a challenge. This is why I say that it's great when the department is cohesive and supportive, because he says that that's the way we were for him. He came to us and said, "You won't believe this class. What am I going to do with these kids?" So we started talking about the kinds of things that were going to happen. Here this White man has this almost 100 percent Black class. I said, "The first thing they're going to say when you clamp down on them is 'You're prejudiced' and so now you've got to be prepared to deal with that." We went through all the things that could happen, and I said, "It must be going through the back of your mind, 'Why all these kids? Why just those kids?'" He said, "Yes, I really wanted to ask that." I said, "Go ahead, ask anything you want. We're not sensitive to anything. We think we understand the problem."

To make a long story short, Jerry changed those children's lives. He had kids coming to class who had never been to class since the first week of school. Some of them I think he wished he had left where they were. He was creative. For every problem that they presented to him, he found a solution.

He worked at it; it was not easy at all. You would just not have believed the change in those kids.

Now, here is a teacher who is competent in subject matter, math background. We don't get them often. He could teach almost any subject, I think, in high school. He got involved in math clubs and the extra activities. We spend a lot of time in the resource center at lunchtime and after school, and he came right on in there spending his lunchtime with us and after school until 4:30.

At the end of the school year, when they started drawing up programs, there was no place for him, yet at one of the other high schools there was a position that's mainly remedial, practical math and general math. He went for the interview and told me, "I don't want to be stuck in a position where I can't grow. If the members of the department are going to say, 'On the basis of seniority, you get to teach the algebra, geometry, and trig and this,' then I don't want it." When he went to the interview, they offered him a program that included one geometry class, with the possibility, but no guarantee, that it would look better the next year.

The last time I talked with him he was mulling over whether he should accept this position, and I told him that he's not obligated to do but one year on this contract; then he can decide. He really wants to be a teacher, and he really is good at it. He teaches folk dancing. One day we heard this music at lunch time. We heard all this clapping, and I thought, "This is just great. What a wonderful way to get kids to let down their inhibitions and to see you as human."

No Excuses

I think teachers have to learn about kids whose backgrounds are different. The thing that was different about Jerry was that he knew, he understood that people are people. One group will accuse you of doing things to them that you don't do to other people, and if you aren't doing that, you don't worry about it. You don't offer excuses for why you're here. You say, "Look, there's nothing wrong with your mind. This is what we're going to do today. Go ahead and do it." Then as relationships improve the students can have more input.

He was like that and they understood. He was the teacher and he was in charge. He was not afraid of them. He did not expect them to do anything that any other students didn't do. If they did, they could expect repercussions from him; he wasn't going to tolerate misbehavior.

Professionalism and Classroom Reality

I see some hope for the teaching profession. Beginning salaries are more attractive. When the state gets rid of the permanent credential that allows districts to keep people who are not prepared to teach, there will be vacancies for people who are new to the profession.

One of the other problems is teacher education. I can only speak for California now. I don't think that people who go through teacher education programs have a good feel for what the job really requires of them. It's all right to do student teaching, especially if they get a chance to see beyond their own classrooms, but I don't think that there's enough input from people who are in the profession. I ask my student teachers if, in their seminars, they invite real teachers to come back and participate, and apparently not a lot do.

The thing that I liked about having Jerry interning was that I could say, "I bet you have some wonderful stories to tell your seminar group when you go back to class." He said he really did, and he didn't think he would ever have had that perspective without being in the classroom. He doesn't think that anybody could have told him what to expect or how to deal with it. If he had not wanted to consult with us, he did not have to, but he chose to. He felt that this was the thing that made him really decide, "I can do this job. There aren't any problems that I can't handle."

MESA and the Money Crunch

I've been thinking that my school district could never pay me what I'm worth, but I don't have any bitterness about that. I was talking with the assistant superintendent for instruction, because there are going to be some reductions in the size of MESA.[8] I think she knows that even if there is no compensation for it, we are always going to have a MESA program as long as I am there. Yet at the same time, that's no excuse for not providing whatever resources the school district can provide.

I don't want anybody to feel that there is an excuse, so I do say to them, "I put in as much time as the basketball coach and the football coach combined. I do this all year long." I keep reminding them. The assistant superintendent knows; she really embraces the program. She used to be the principal at my school. All the school districts are in a money crunch, but MESA is saying to the school districts, "OK, we are in a money crunch too, and you've got to do something to help supply some of the services." I don't know what their contributions will be, but I will still be there.

Teacher as Role Model

I can only speak from the Black perspective; I remember when the teacher could do no wrong. The teacher was never challenged. Now I don't think that's good, but I'm saying that's the extent of the confidence that the parents and community had in the teacher. A teacher accused of lying? My parents would have killed me if I had even said that. They would have known that it wasn't true.

Historically the teacher has been a special person. I don't think the community should be unreasonable in its expectations but I think it's reasonable for them to expect that if you're going to be exposed to these kids all day you're going to influence them in positive ways. You're not going to be out there doing all those things that you're telling them they shouldn't do.

Remember what I said, kids are still kids, they are not adults. As young adults, they should have some responsibilities, but they are still basically kids and while yes, they are still responsible for their actions, they've got to have good role models. All the people who want to be teachers aren't good role models any more.

There used to be things that teachers did not dare do because the larger community didn't allow it. Well, we're so big now it's different, but some of these attitudes still come through. The negative ones seem to stand out, way out. The kids pick up on them and so then they no longer see the teacher as a special person in their lives, but just like everybody else.

I don't want to be treated that way. I'm special in their lives and I want to be special. I had a student who never called me by my name. She always called me "Teacher." Even now, she's graduated but she still calls me Teacher. Whenever she sees me she says, "Hi Teacher," with a very warm feeling when she says it.

Notes

[1] Sarah Lawrence Lightfoot, "The Lives of Teachers," in *Handbook of Teaching and Policy*, eds. Lee S. Shulman and Gary Sykes (N.Y.: Longman, Inc. 1983), p. 242.

[2] Bay Area Writing Project, 5627 Tolman Hall, University of California, Berkeley, CA 94720.

3 The Math Solution, Marilyn Burns Education Associates, 150 Gate 5 Road, Suite 101, Sausalito, CA 94965; California Math Leadership Program, Alameda County Office of Education, 313 West Winton Avenue, Hayward, CA 94544.

4 California Assessment Program, *A Question of Thinking, A First Look at Students' Performance on Open-ended Questions in Mathematics* (Sacramento, CA: Calif. Dept. of Education, 1989).

5 See p. 149 for an explanation of the FAMILY MATH program.

6 Teachers had little difficulty in identifying Proposition 13 and the weakness of the districts' funding base as the immediate cause of layoffs, actual and threatened. Even before Proposition 13 in 1978 and the lottery in 1984, teachers recognized problems attendant on school funding, and the link between funding sources and autonomy. Local districts hoped to develop a balanced mix of federal, state, and local funds. Their intent was to preserve a measure of autonomy and financial control without jeopardizing state support designed to equalize school funding across districts. In 1977, before Proposition 13, the state's contribution to the support of public primary and secondary education was substantial (about 42 percent), but its share was not preponderant. In 1979, a year after the passage of Prop. 13, the state's share of funding had increased to 68 percent. As state funding grew, local school districts felt their own autonomy declining. See Ronald J. Heckart and Terry J. Dean, *Proposition 13 in the 1978 California Primary: A Post-Election Bibliography* (Berkeley: Institute of Governmental Studies Library, University of California, 1981), p. 79.

Advocates of Prop. 13 argued that overburdened property taxpayers needed relief, and that the proposition was designed to benefit householders caught in the spiral of inflationary increases in the value of their property. The growth in state control of educational funding was not a signal feature of the pro-arguments. Nevertheless the shift to greater state control surfaced as an unintended consequence that teachers recognized in the dreaded March 15 "possible layoff" notices.

The electorate's tinkering with school funding continued in 1979 when state Proposition 4 (the Gann limit) controlled state spending—including spending for public education—through a formula based on population increases and the national Consumer Price Index. (Over a decade later, Proposition 111, June 1990, set a more generous new formula that included population growth but exchanged the national index for the percentage growth in California personal income.)

In 1989 the state's Proposition 98 guaranteed that increasing percentages of the state budget would support schools and community colleges. In one way, this move looked good from the schools' point of view, but it set the schools as adversaries to an array of other significant state functions and funding responsibilities. In yet another change of direction, in 1991 newly elected Governor Pete Wilson announced that, because of the state's deficit, Proposition 98's funds would be subject to challenge.

7 The lottery raised troubling issues about the quality of the public's commitment to public education, and of the ethics and propriety of relying on gambling to share the support of public education. Still unsolved are questions of 1) whether the lottery

funds enrich through augmentation, 2) displace regular long-term state funding, or 3) contribute significantly toward boosting revenues overall.

Part of the lottery debate turns on whether those funds are used to enhance or augment programs, or whether they are to be viewed as "regular" funding for education. While the 1984 act specifically prohibits the Legislature from substituting lottery money for funds from general taxes, efforts soon began to find ways to circumvent that prohibition.

Public perception of the role played by lottery funds adds to the confusion. Len Feldman of the CTA has commented that every time the public sees a lottery ad with the slogan "our schools win too," there is an implication that the lottery is providing for public education, so that more tax money is no longer needed. Cecelia Chan, "Lottery bonanza only a drop in education bucket" (*California Journal*, June 1986, 295 and 297.)

A number of school superintendents also expressed their concern that while lottery revenues were failing to keep up with enrollment growth, the public was receiving the message that lottery revenues should be regarded as another revenue source for basic aid for public education. Eric Hartwig, *Do "Our Schools Win Too?" School Uses of Lottery Revenues: Year One*, Policy Paper No. PP 877-4-7 (Berkeley: PACE [Policy Analysis for California Education], University of California, April 1987) note 30, p. 33.

[8] MESA is the Mathematics, Science, Engineering Achievement program, headquartered at the Lawrence Hall of Science. The program works to increase the number of minority students prepared to enroll in science and engineering majors in college. Contact Fred Easter, Director, MESA, Lawrence Hall of Science, University of California, Berkeley, CA 94720.

Part 3

A PLACE FOR ADVENTURERS

Learning is at the heart of good teaching, and the ways children learn hold endless fascination for adventurous teachers. The more these teachers find out about the learning process, the more they want to know.

To teach well involves honoring children's perceptions, seeing the learning process through their eyes, and understanding the stages of development through which each child passes. Consequently, teachers need freedom to experiment with the physical and intellectual conditions of teaching. They know how closely the two freedoms are linked in the classroom. Freedom to to pursue an exciting idea and freedom to arrange space, together multiply the opportunities for teaching and learning.

Teachers who focus on the ways children learn often find traditional classrooms and prescribed methods uncomfortable for theselves and unproductive for their students. For Bob Whitlow and Nan Jackson, it was necessary to find teaching positions out of the mainstream. Both were able to create hospitable environments where they could use all of their talents.

Bob Whitlow

Nan Jackson

Bob Whitlow:
Teachers and Parents, a Wary Partnership

Finding the Focus

I almost immediately realized I could have fun being a teacher. I could play, I could be creative, and I could act. I was in a lot of drama in school, and I still get to do that. I can follow my interests and continue to be a learner; that's one of the things that makes me feel good about myself as a teacher. I feel bad sometimes that I'm not well organized or that I don't have the scope and sequence down perfectly. But what I do give my kids is a strong enthusiasm for learning.

I essentially flunked my junior and senior years in high school in math, and I know why. I had a good math aptitude and still do, but I did not do well in math because the teaching was so bad. I have a strong memory about my emotions as a young person, and the frustration that comes when good teaching is denied to you.

I went to college in the late 60s, and graduated in 1971 from UC Santa Barbara. By the time I was in my senior year, I didn't care any more. My grades were getting better, but Vietnam was still very real. I was politically aware, and excited, and vehement. My brother was flying jets in Vietnam, and I had been pushed out of the family for my views on that war.

I went to college—like all good White boys from Southern California—as a pre-med major. I was going to study and be a good student. It didn't last long. I barely passed chemistry with a C. I passed calculus with a C, but I couldn't answer any questions on the final. Next quarter I started chem lab and spilled silver nitrate all over a new shirt that my grandmother had given me, and I dropped out of that class the next day. I went into a class that my neighbor in the dorm was taking that excited him. It was a class on Christianity—Evil in a Good World—or something like that. I ended up being a religious studies major. I thought strongly about seminary, and a lot of that had to do with my growing political consciousness and feelings about what needed to be done to change things.

There were a number of things that began to focus for me at the end of my college career, and one of them was that I definitely was not going to go the road my dad did. He's a recently retired lawyer in Orange County. I had a political and world view opposite from his. It wasn't just a reaction to my parents, but that was part of it.

I got a job cleaning houses, living in a swamp. Finally, I decided to go to Cal State Hayward and get my teaching credential. I found myself the iconoclast in all my education classes, because I still wanted to play, and I was not going to let go of my anti-establishment viewpoint. Some teachers really liked me, others did not. In one class I had everybody in the class, all 25 of us, turn in one final. We all came over to my house, we wrote the best final that anybody could have possibly ever written for that class, and turned it in. Everybody got an A except me, I got a B. I didn't know it at the time, but I was doing cooperative learning.

Teacher as a Student, Learning from Teachers

In my education classes, student training was not very well handled, except for one teacher, Dale Hendrickson, who taught language arts. He was on fire, as four or five other professors in my life have been. He told stories all the time, oral presentations of short stories, and had a file of 3 x 5 cards, reminding him what the story was about. He had 6,000 stories in his head, and encouraged us to do the same thing. You didn't sleep in his class. You had to come up with a card file of your own, so you had to read short stories like crazy. He's one more guy who showed me how you could be a teacher.

I went into my first student teaching experience not really knowing anything. It was right down the street from where I lived. The principal happened to be a guy that now I know pretty well. He took one look at my ponytail and said, "I think you should go with this teacher"; he must have thought there was only one teacher on the staff who would be able to handle me. The teacher was young and, if she modelled anything, it was that she was energetic and had a good attitude with her kids. They had a good attitude with her. That's more important than any curriculum or tricks of the trade. I got that from her.

That summer I got a long-term substitute job in a preschool, which was really neat for me because these little three-year-olds would come up and drool on my knee. In my family I don't ever remember a hug. Ever. This taught me some lessons about affection and kids.

Teachers as Inspiration

In my first year of teaching, Myrtle Chapman was the 6th grade teacher down the hall from me. Myrtle Chapman was 65 years old, always wore a high-collared blouse with a brooch and a coat, and carried a megaphone in the recess yard. She had the best-behaved 6th graders I've ever seen in my life. They did the neatest activities. They loved Mrs. Chapman. This was her year of retirement, and she stayed every day, until 5:00 or 6:00, just as I did. She was an inspiration to me. She was a very strict teacher but she loved those kids. I hardly ever talked to her, but I learned a lot from her personality.

There was also a young woman who taught across the hall from me, who was very open about helping me learn. One of the things I learned from her was how to get a form out of the office. I didn't even know you had to have forms. Nobody told me anything. The district didn't give any kind of packet of information. Over the next two or three years, as we taught in the same school together, I gleaned a lot from her. She was a strict, traditional teacher in many ways, but she really cared about her kids and worked hard, overtime. I had a number of teachers who were attractive to me as people, as personalities, as friends in my life.

Lyle Lewinson was my 6th grade teacher, and I owe him a lot. I was always the leader in my class, and quite comfortable and confident with that, but there were some roles that needed to be played. I had to please my parents, and I had to please my teachers to the point where, just in the last year, I have enough confidence not to try to make everybody happy.

Leadership

There was a group of parents who had established a cooperative nursery school in Hayward and didn't want to let go.* They were a hippie group; the program was founded with strong principles about Indians and stewardship of the earth, and basically anti-establishment points of view. It took them two years to organize. They brought a proposal before the school board that wasn't accepted. Then one of the parents, who is still working at the county level, helped them write a proposal. They kept going back to the school board until they finally got their proposal—for a classroom within the school—accepted.

---

*For information on the Hayward Unified School District population, see note on p. 5.

When I heard about the job with this weird school, I went and interviewed; I wore work boots and a cowboy shirt and didn't shave. There were nine parents on the panel; they liked me, they liked my energy.

They had a classroom of about 28 kids the first year, and the next year they wanted to expand so they hired me. That year was volatile. The parent meetings consisted of screaming and crying, and there was no leadership. I was new. I mostly just sat there. The other teacher was good about making sure that I was equal, but she was not interested in taking any kind of leadership role. This was the parents' program, she felt, and they were running it, and she was just the teacher.

By the third year of the program, which was my second year, she was gone and we were back down to 28 kids and I was the only teacher. There was a lot of this going on: "I want it this way"; "No, I want it this way." I quickly said, "I'm going to be the leader of this classroom and this is the way we're going to do things. If you've got another idea, great." There were several of the founding parents who were quite disenchanted with that. It was definitely trial by fire, and I read my *I Ching* a lot, which is a book about leadership.[1] That's what it's about. Leadership and people.

In those early days when I first got my own classroom, I had to sell the program. Anybody who came in, I grabbed and I said, "Listen ....." I was selling them and I was selling me. I couldn't give all the parents what they wanted. Those that were saying, "We don't want any structure for our kids," had to leave; and those saying, "We want workbooks every day," had to leave.

It was devastating to me to lose kids because I needed to make everybody happy. It really hurt me. If Hitler were to walk in that room and say, "I'm not happy with you," I'd feel bad. I was single and lived within a few blocks of school and I was there a lot. I had an average of two or three phonecalls a night from parents. I just took it all on. It took me years to get away from that.

That first year by myself we had an administration that was bound and determined to crush that program, to "bring it back into the mainstream of the school district's educational policy." I survived by the skin of my teeth, and by having parents behind me. We united against a common enemy on the outside, the administration. We were the only alternative classroom within a completely traditional school. We were, in fact, a school within a school. Parents from all over the district had chosen this class for their children, and some were even outside of the district.

Parents Teaching in the Program

Somehow I've been able to weave it into my personal and professional philosophy that you must have parents actively teaching in the program, no matter how difficult it is. If that is a given, if it's the life breath of the program, then just have it. Put up with it. It pays off. It goes both ways too. These parents get to see how hard my job is. The parents are interacting with the kids, they're learning a lot about each other, and the whole family unit is richer for it. We are all richer for it. Instead of waving bye-bye to your 5-year-old the day that he goes off to kindergarten, or the day that she starts 1st grade, you get to interact in school.

One of my parents started writing a book on alternative education. She went around to alternative programs in the Bay Area that were supposedly "parent-active" programs, and she found that sooner or later the parents are weeded out of the program, because it's a pain. I could be a more efficient teacher if I were doing all the teaching. One could think that my kids would be learning more and they would be more on task.

In my program, our overriding philosophy is that we're here to nurture our kids. For the most part, the parents trust each other's judgment. For those parents who can't be in the classroom program, they know that the great majority of people in that program are there because they really love the program and the kids, and that those kids are going to be getting a healthy, nurturing environment.

Parents' Reward

Over the years there have been many attempts to legislate parent involvement: "You must put in one day a week or you're out of the program." Well, that's not how I work. There are a lot of programs that are like this; people come from parent coop nursery schools that have strict rules about attendance and meetings. But I know that unless people really want to be there, even if you make them be there, they're not worth it. Those people who are in there are really good, and those people who don't want to be there, aren't there. Those that are in between are in between. It's just that loose and fluid. I have people who have been working in my classroom ever since I've been there, for 14 years.

One parent has been teaching in my class for eight years and she's just finishing a teaching credential. She came in as a housewife with a five-year-old and a nursing baby. She learned that she has some strong skills. Working with the kids, she's the energetic and intelligent kind of person who found herself by being a teacher. She'll finish up her credential this year and they will be dying to get her on the staff because she's an excellent teacher. There are several other people who have done the same thing or are in the process of it.

It is a program that is just as much for parents as it is for kids. It's a strong support group. It was getting to the point where we had a long waiting list, so we expanded. Norma was hired four years ago, and then we had 65 kids in three rooms. With that we gained more people and more power, and lost family a little bit. Then last year we expanded again and Amy [now replaced by Karen] came on the staff, and so now we have 90 kids and three of us full-time in the program, plus all the parents.

Who Fits, and Who Believes

There are kids who don't fit here. It's not a structured classroom. There is not a place for every kid. You can't look around and see that somebody's out and away from the desk—there are no desks. So the child who is just wild, who is overstimulated by this kind of environment, has to leave. That's happened five times in the last 14 years. The child whose parent does not buy into this system has to leave. Those parents want more "show" in the academic realm: "I want to see that homework. I don't believe they're getting it."

I struggle to this day with alternative ways of teaching. We had a major blowout in class a couple of weeks ago, because some of the 2nd grade parents wanted to get tutors for their kids. The next door kid was "reading," but their kid wasn't. "When's my kid going to learn to read?" I said, "Honest, listen to me. I'm not lying to you. This is a better way."

How do you convince a parent whose ego is on the line, to whom Mrs. Jones from next door says, "Listen, my Johnny reads the socks off your Susie." This parent has every right to worry, so I constantly give inservice to my parents. I have a whole bank of articles that I run past these people all the time, and a bibliography.

When somebody has a question about something, I've got a bibliography with 40 entries and more to give to this person. I say, "Read this, will you? Please believe me, and just wait." I have confessions from parents, "Well, when my son was in 2nd grade, I felt the same way." So I continually have to sell it, but now I don't have to sell myself any more.

Parents' Meetings and Arguments

At every parent meeting, or at least every other parent meeting—we have them every six weeks—an argument comes up. I've heard the argument before. I don't know which of the 12 arguments this happens to be, but the same thing goes on and on and these people have to work their way through it. I sit there and I let them work their way through it. They argue about participation, or they argue about this or they argue about that, and they all have to have something to say and they all get a chance to say it because Bob sits there and waits through it.

The parents, for the most part, are in every week; not every kid's parents, of course. There are many parents who do not come into the classroom. Many of them are teachers, and they can't work it in. So, mostly they don't know what is going on; they just trust us. They are free to call me any time, and they do. They all come to parent conferences. They get to pack every question they've got into 20 minutes, and I've got to get everybody's packed into 20 minutes, 15 times a day. (The other teachers share this with me.)

Rewards of Democracy

I run meetings really well, and parent meetings are not easy to run. You've got to know when to cut people off, and whom to call on, and where you're going. I'm really good at time. If a meeting is going to be over at two minutes to nine, it's over at three minutes to nine. I've let others run the meetings now, and some of them go on and on and on. That's been a hard one for me to let go.

You have to be true to yourself and what you believe in, and persevere. It may take a long time, but if you're honest about where you're going, things will come to you. You have to share the power. A wise person doesn't take it all on.

When we have a parent meeting we have 50 or 60 people. One of my overriding philosophies about this whole deal is democracy, and it's inefficient. You've got all these different people. But from a teaching standpoint, you've got all these different personalities interacting. I couldn't come up with so many ideas. Judy does science every Monday and Sherry does it every Tuesday. Daryl is a chiropractor and he comes in and builds bodies; Jack is a director at the YMCA and he comes in and does P. E.; and Roxanne's an artist.

[John, Norma, Karen, and Bob are teachers on the staff. All the other adults are parent volunteers.] A kid could go to read literature, short stories for about a half hour or so, then either go down to play sports with Jack, which is a very popular thing to do, or to one of the mini centers that are being offered throughout the week. It's his own choice.

He or she could have made muscles out of balloons and paper with Daryl, or could have gone to the writing center, or to science, or with Sherry and Harry Smith who have invented a game called the "The Land of Blue Sky." It's very much like Dungeons and Dragons. Each kid gets to pick a character and traits that go with that character. The whole Land of Blue Sky has to get together somehow to learn how to build and grow this crystal to shoot the meteor and blow it out of the sky to save the Land of Blue Sky by June. These two parents come every Tuesday. Sherry stays the whole day. Harry leaves at noon because he still has to put in his eight hours at a big computer concern, so on Tuesday he works until 8 o'clock at night. On Tuesday they are Redbeard and Alpha. They don't go by their real names because they're from the Land of the Blue Sky.

Each one of the centers is staffed by a parent, unless a kid brings in a center that he or she wants to set up. There are tons of things going on. Jeannie was out measuring bodies in the hallway; I don't know what she was doing. I don't always know what's going on.

The parents are different every day. Monday afternoons, Maureen and Anne are language arts parents, and they would do writing activities. Tuesday afternoons the parents are Sherry and Daryl and they do science. It goes like that.

I couldn't duplicate it. I sit there somewhere in the middle and try to funnel people through, and be as responsive as I can to the kids' needs—and try to remember that that's why school exists. The other school, the traditional school, is structured and organized for the convenience of adults. It's that simple. Otherwise they wouldn't put all the seven-year-olds in one room. It's detrimental to their health.

Running the Program and Rotating Responsibilities

We do a lot sitting on the rug in the classroom, especially in the morning. People have a lot of things to share, and we don't always get to all of them. Kids usually bring things in a bag; they have the initials of each thing, like, "Yesterday I had A A A F C M F B." It's something like "An Awesome Award From *Cricket Magazine* For Beth." Beth, one of my students, had won an award from *Cricket Magazine* for writing a story. That's the kind of thing. Then we would take attendance, and maybe the kids would read a news article. We have a lot of parents who volunteer to teach on certain days, so those who are teaching today would say what they are doing.

While all this is going on, I'm sitting in the corner like this, with my hands over my ears. Yesterday, for the first hour I was trying to organize my life. I wasn't teaching. I had been gone for three days, but I had the luxury of doing that. I find myself doing that more often than most teachers do, because I'm basically running more than a classroom.

Normally I would be working with small groups of children. On a typical Tuesday morning I would be working with the 2nd graders in reading. After break from 10 to 10:15, they all have a snack together out in the yard, and then it is my turn to rotate.

Today I took a group to room 7 and we worked on our reading contracts all morning. This month they all got to choose their own books. They have to write three character sketches, two setting sketches, and then choose from other kinds of writing activities. At the end they are going to present their books by doing a commercial, interviewing a character, coming in costume, and so on.

Yesterday there was an assembly, which took up the rest of the afternoon. On a normal Tuesday afternoon a 4th grader would either be with me in a group that was 3rd to 4th graders mixed together, or with another teacher. There's a child safety curriculum that I have been doing in the afternoon. It's out of Seattle and it's along the lines of "Strong, Safe, and Free." I'm big on that kind of stuff.

Tracing one kid through the day is difficult. Kids can get lost, or not do anything, and so we get together and say, "What's with this kid? Is she doing anything?" I have my hands on those older kids almost every day so I can see how they're doing. I don't give report cards. I don't give norm-referenced tests as we go through. I just kind of have to go by sense of touch on how they're doing.

Creating a Strong Curriculum and Knowing How Children Learn

One of the reasons my test scores are good is that these kids belong to parents who care a lot about their education, and they'd probably do well anywhere. The other reason is that we have a really good curriculum and a really good understanding of how children learn, and learn better. My 2nd grade reading scores are low, because reading tests are all phonics-based. My

5th grade reading scores are, on the average, two years above grade-level because my reading program is founded on meaning and real reading.

Real reading takes longer to achieve. Kids who can read aloud to their parents in the 1st grade are not really reading; they're making sounds. Great. You can train a dog to jump through a hoop and you can train a kid to make sounds off the page, but if he gets caught up in that as the foundation of his reading he will always read slowly, word for word. Chances are he might not enjoy reading because it's a slow process. In fact, he'll be just like me. I'm not a reader, and I'm very slow.

If 1st graders are expected to learn to read, then you're taking a huge percentage of kids and saying, "You are going to fail." Do you know that kids fail kindergarten? Well, that's stupid. In Europe and the Soviet Union they don't worry about "reading" until the kids are older. So in my program I get kids whose parents are worried that they're not reading yet in 2nd grade, but they've got a strong language base. They can tell stories and they can do plays and they write with older partners.

It's so much fun for some of these kids in the 3rd and 4th grades, they go bing! and they're reading in a week. It's within a week, and it's just incredible. They put it all together. If you screw them up or make them hate reading or worry about it or bend them around a little bit at five or six years old, they may never go bing! They'll get it, like I got it, but they won't love it. We'll be discussing part of a book, and I'll say, "All right, read to the end of the page." I'll finish and I'll look up and they're all waiting for me to finish, because they're all fast. They process text in a different way than I do, because I haven't slowed them down. I don't know if I've taught them or if I've just left them alone. That's another part of good teaching: knowing when to back off and just leave them alone.

Probably my strongest teaching technique is the question. If you want to know if a child understands what she's reading, ask her questions about it. Instead of doing a workbook, why not take all that time, sit back and just talk about it. "Gee, we've got a story about cats here. Have you got a cat at home? Tell me about your cat, what do you think about that?" Build up, model how you approach thinking. Model how you approach the text, and expand this child's world from the outside.

Wonder and Flexibility

When people ask what I get from my students, the first thing that comes to mind is that it's a lot of fun. I enjoy every day. I don't dread going to work. Sometimes I dread getting up, but not very much. Many more days than not

I go to school with not a whole lot planned: "I wonder what's going to happen today."

I have overriding things that I'm trying to get done. We worked on our reading contracts today and I have the math menu, but the nature of the program is such that I have to play it by ear. Over the years, people have asked me for specific lesson plans or things laid out in a certain order, and I've tried, but I can't. I can't because there are so many people involved that you never know from one minute to the next who's going to show up, and with what.

Yesterday, Alice, a parent, came in. She is the first oboe in the San Jose Symphony. She played some Bach on the piano and the oboe. We took 40 minutes out of our day and we sat around and did that. She wasn't scheduled to come in but she called and said, "I can do it if you want." I'm not going to turn her away.

Satisfactions

Today we had a discussion about two words: "moral" and "value." I'm bound and determined to talk about morals and values. When I talk about values—when I start on the Indians—the kids go, "Oh, my God. He's talking about the Indians again." So it's been a truth in my program: I get to preach. We talk about feelings a lot, and maybe what I get to do is be the father that I didn't have, because the kids can come to me. I'm physical with my kids constantly. We touch and we hug, and so I enjoy teaching. I get to give back.

The other thing that I get from my kids is my opportunity to grow and develop. What I give to them is an attitude about learning—I hope, and an attitude about living—I hope. Parents have to make a decision, and in the earlier years of the program it was more difficult because I was the only teacher in these children's lives for five years, kindergarten through 4th grade. The parents were choosing a teacher. That was quite a burden to bear too; what if I was screwing these kids up? I have a certain kind of personality that some people, I guess, wouldn't like and some people obviously did because they stuck with the program. So, yes, there's ego in there. I get to be an influence on these children's lives.

Validation and Self-Questioning

Several years ago, I realized I needed to stop working in a vacuum; I needed some theory. I knew that what I was doing was working, but people want it in black and white, so I went to Cal to get my Master's. At Cal they were saying, "What? You what? Can we see this?" They'd come to my class and they'd say, "Wow, this is great. This is fabulous. This is just what we need." I'd say, "Write a letter to my superintendent, will you?" So I started reaching out professionally.

I got very strong validation for what I was doing, and they liked me. I ended up getting an award when I graduated for the outstanding something-or-other. My friend Rick McCallum, who got his Ph.D. last year, did his dissertation work in my classroom.[2] It's up for dissertation of the year, nationally. So now I have hard copy on why my program works.

To Stay or to Leave

One of the big, huge things wrong in education is the isolation of teachers: people working in their own little cubicles with one grade-level of kids. It goes against everything we know about working or succeeding or learning. Over the years, I have invited people in to my classroom to see what I'm doing. Most teachers just kind of sit back and say, "Hey, where are the desks? What's going on here? I could never do this. How could you have parents in your room? There's no learning going on here. It's too noisy." Those are the negatives.

A couple of teachers come in now and say, "Do you have anything on this?" Or, "What do you think about that?" Of course, you're never hot stuff in your own backyard. I was a mentor teacher for two years and I tried, but people didn't want it.[3] People have their own agendas.

There were times when I wanted to quit, early on. I remember breaking down in front of my principal in my third year. I said, "I can't take it any more." I didn't want to start another year of this stuff, it was so difficult and I was young. I don't know what kept me going. Maybe I was afraid to quit. I really believed in what I was doing. Part of it was ego; I couldn't let it go. Now it's certainly deeper than that. There's still some ego there, but I have to share that program with so many more people now, it's not just my baby. I have to let Karen have her way and Norma have her way, and work in between. But professionally now I see that I can do anything I want to. I've got K–6 kids, real parent involvement, and all the innovative curriculum I can handle.

Every time I think about leaving, it's hard for me. I've got the ideal teaching situation. I am on the cutting edge right now. I don't have to say to anybody, "when I was teaching." I am a classroom teacher right now and that's important to me. That comes under the category of being honest and straightforward with my peers. I would leave because I don't want to get stale. I would leave because I want a new challenge, or I might find an arena where I could be more effective.

If I do leave it will be a heart-wrenching experience for me. Whenever I'm out of my classroom I start feeling out of sorts. I start feeling—not guilty— but I've lost contact with my students. There's not the continuity. I would like to coordinate curriculum development in our school district, and again, have some such teacher in every school. We need to have an innovative curriculum.

In every school there needs to be some kind of master teacher whose business it is to follow up new goals for the district. If you're going to do math inservices, then there has to be somebody back at the site who goes around the next day and says, "Does anybody have any questions? Can I get any materials for anybody? Can I come into your classroom and demonstrate? Is there anything you need?" It doesn't exist, but it's good management. They do it in the private sector, I'm sure.

There are a couple of books I'd like to write, and there's lots of curriculum I've generated for my own classroom. I've written stuff over the years, just tons and tons of stuff that goes into the waste basket when I'm done with it. It's illustrated and thoughtfully produced. I have a very sound theory background. I know why these pieces work here and they don't work there, and I don't have the time to write the books.

Changes and Artistry

There need to be some wholesale changes in the way schools are set up. The whole system is poorly structured, especially for the present day we live in. They tried some pretty big changes in the 60s with pod schools. Now all those pod schools have barriers built up and people are back to single classrooms.

I think you have to have a major shift in philosophy about what learning is. Piaget's theories are accepted, but it's just lip service.[4] We're still making five-year-old kids learn things that only nine-year-olds can learn. So there has to be a major commitment from the top down on long-range changes in philosophy and curriculum. In this country, we have such a short-sighted view of how things are to be accomplished. We need some way to maintain, from the top down, something consistent over 25 years, and then you have to work from the bottom up.

It is critical that people coming out of teacher education schools have at least experienced the alternative teaching style. As a mentor teacher a couple of years ago, I had to sit through six full days of clinical supervision and Bloom's Taxonomy again. This is what they're doing in schools now. They're judging teachers and making everybody do the lockstep fashion of a lesson plan.

I'm sure you can take something valuable out of anybody's system, but we are essentially cutting it into little pieces again and making it "teacher proof." We're taking the artistry out of teaching. It's an art. It is a feeling. It is something that's soft and warm, and we're making it hard and cold.

We need to encourage people to do what they think is right, which involves a lot of self knowledge and confidence. I don't know how you attract those kinds of people unless you let them know that programs like this one exist and that teaching is a profession that allows this kind of innovation. That means they need access to people like me. They don't have to spend their whole student teaching experience in a program like mine, but one quarter would be nice. They'd get to see K through 6. They'd get to listen to me talk at them constantly.

After reading his transcript, Bob Whitlow sent in these further thoughts:

"I made the decision to become a teacher back in the wide-eyed idealism of the late 60s and early 70s. It was a political choice. I thought I could make a difference. I was an optimist. Most of us are that way in our twenties. Now I'm a little scared that optimism is dying. I look around at those walls that I once thought were crumbling and they seem to be higher and stronger than ever. And it seems that there are fewer of us around to try to scale them.

"On the grand scale—the nation and the world—I don't see things turning around. It's odd. For an optimist I'm very pessimistic right now. I will continue to work for change on the local level. I think it is still possible although I realize more and more how difficult and slight the changes are. Depends on what day it is. I just love my students. They are so fresh and alive with fun and curiosity. I just don't want their future taken from them by some faceless system motivated by profit over humanity.

"I think maybe I see a crack in the wall over there."

Nan Jackson: Learning by Teaching

A House Full of Books

Our house always seemed full of books accessible to us to explore. I always got a sense of my parents being interested in a lot of different things: not only science for my father (he's a physicist), but art as well, and, for my mother, English and French, literature and poetry.

It was a supportive environment; they were obviously interested in what we were doing at school. Having the four children so close together in age made a big difference because we would help each other. During high school, I did a lot of reading of English literature through my older brother's interest and recommendations. I remember helping my younger sister with math. In a sense, there was a lot of informal teaching among the kids, which I think has a lot to do with my sense of teaching. It could have been very different if I were the only child.

We went to public schools. This was important to my parents. During my 5th grade year we took a sabbatical and I went to an international school, with classes in English. I had a great teacher who had a lot to do with my excitement about learning. He was obviously talented and interested in many fields, and I associate him with math and poetry, which have become very important to me. He encouraged me in math, and towards the end of the year he tried to introduce me to algebra. I remember feeling how useless it was and wondering why he was so keen on getting me to understand things that seemed so obvious; associative, commutative, and distributive properties. Later, when I had some algebra, I could think back and see exactly what he was trying to get me to do—a little too early.

The Excitement of Math, the Terror of Chemistry

The classes I remember most were math classes, with the excitement, and all the students being interested in learning. One class I remember in particular was experimental. It was in vector algebra, which we did in an abstract way. Every single day we proved a bunch of theorems. The teacher would write the theorem up on the board and the class would start coming up with steps, all algebraic. She wrote extremely quickly on the board but still couldn't keep up with all the students. It was this intense excitement for 50 minutes that stuck in my mind. The whole class was participating with her and she was excited and enthusiastic about what she was doing.

All in all, I'd say my education was quite good, but I wanted to get out of high school so much that I graduated at the end of summer in my junior year. My family was going to go back to Europe in December and I thought I could go with them for half a year. It also sticks in my mind that if I stayed I would have to take chemistry, and I was scared of chemistry. I also felt very intimidated by the high-powered English courses I would have had to jump into. Since I had gone to summer school, I had enough credits, and I decided to graduate, much to my father's dismay. One day I said to him, "Could you give me a ride down to the high school on your way to work? I'd like to pick up my diploma." He had no idea that I was even thinking about graduating.

College, and the Romance of Geology

During the fall of what would have been my senior year, I audited some courses at Cal in French and studied math on my own so that I could take the SAT [Scholastic Aptitude Test]. In subtle ways, that contributed some to my teaching, having done a whole course just from a book, going through and doing every single problem and actually having a great time doing that.

In college I took an undergraduate degree in geology and intended to become a geologist, but talking to professors in the Ph.D. program, who told me what kind of research I could do, seemed to shrivel all of my interest into some narrow place. I didn't know anything about geology as a profession. It was mainly through a lot of backpacking and hiking experiences and taking a first geology course that I got excited about being in a profession where I could be out in the field, mapping the world, that kind of thing. It was a very romantic vision.

Peace Corps: Teaching in Morocco

The Peace Corps offered my first teaching experience. I got into the Peace Corps partly as an alternative to graduate school, partly to get back into mathematics through teaching, after doing my degree in geology. At that point, I wasn't expecting to stay in teaching beyond the two-year commitment I made to stay in Morocco.

I was completely unprepared for my first teaching experience. I knew French enough to teach, but I jumped in cold. (In the public high school where I taught, math was taught in French, not Arabic.) During those first few weeks I recognized some of the things I had to do that lasted over two years. I think a lot of how I am as a teacher developed there; those early years were really important for my relationship with my students.

Anxiety and Sympathy in Morocco

Some of the things I learned in those first few months of teaching in Morocco have become comfortable teaching strategies. I was left pretty much on my own, and developed my own style. This might not necessarily have happened if I had gone through a teacher education program. I really value that experience.

At first, I was very frustrated. I remember going home every day and thinking, "I don't really want to go back." At one point I almost went down to look at the mining jobs in the area, a very interesting area geologically. I thought maybe I could do something different, but realized that in a Muslim society it wasn't going to be easy for a woman to get any sort of position out in the field. So I stuck with teaching, and after two months or so became very comfortable with my students.

The students in Morocco were used to a different system from ours, with not much contact with the teacher. Many of the teachers didn't know the students' names, which really shocked me. I remember distinctly the first quiz. It gave me a chance not to be so much on show as the teacher on a pedestal in front of the students. (This was physically true; there was a platform where you were elevated above the students.) I had a chance to go around and look over their shoulders in a sort of inconspicuous way and get to know their names, to get a feeling of who they were. This was the first time I had ever given a test to a group of people and I so strongly felt as if I myself were taking the test; I felt anxious on their behalf. It gave me much more of a feeling of each of them as a person.

I wandered around in the back of the room looking at where I had been lecturing, and suddenly realized that I didn't have to stand up there and talk. The teacher was expected to be up there as a lecturer and obviously that wasn't what I naturally would do.

After that day I knew all the students' names and moved away from lecturing. My knowing their names impressed them. I guess I was able to communicate in French a little better than some of the East European teachers who taught math there and knew their subject well but didn't know

French very well. It also gave me a chance to vary my format from lecturing to involving my students a lot more, involving myself, and just walking around the room.

I had them helping each other, which was something they were used to doing. There was a lot more relaxed interaction among the students in all my classes at that point. I was seeing people after class more. Some students would be having trouble and another student would try to explain, and we would all be working at the board together. Gradually I would step back and watch them teaching and explaining things to each other.

Trying to Study

After two years in Morocco, I enrolled at University College in London in a three-year math program that was for kids coming right out of high school; you took exactly four classes, which were all mathematics and nothing else. I started the second year and then decided to come back to the Bay Area. For a lot of personal reasons, it wasn't a very calm time in my life, and I guess I didn't know what to do. I didn't feel, mid-year, that I could go out and get a teaching job; I didn't have a credential in California.

I applied to Cal as a graduate student in math, struggling through a couple of quarters, doing reasonably well, looking back on it, but at the time I thought I wasn't doing at all well. I missed teaching. I felt very much alone in graduate school in the Math Department. I didn't have friends who understood what I wanted to do or were interested in mathematics so that I could talk about it.

Finally I decided to get back into teaching. Someone was out here interviewing math teachers for a school in St. Croix in the Virgin Islands. It came at the right time, when I had applied for a few geology jobs but had my heart much more in teaching. It was a little like the way I went to Morocco, sort of going partly for the adventure and partly to be back in teaching. When I think about it, the impulse was about the same. That turned out to be a wonderful choice as far as my professional life went. I taught there for three years, and that is when I got a sense of how my colleagues and head master could provide a lot of support professionally. I hadn't had that in Morocco.

One-Person Math Department in St. Croix

I got a chance to know my students well; I was teaching pretty much all of the upper school math courses in a one-person department. There were a number of students who came into my sophomore class and had me as their one math teacher for three years, so I was able to develop quite an attachment to them and have more continuity in my teaching. It might have been nice for them to have seen some other teacher, but the arrangement had advantages too.

That experience made me feel that I might stay in education, and until then I hadn't really thought of it as something permanent for me. Part of that has been a little related to my father and his job. I don't think he ever actually said anything about high school teaching being less worthy than being a professor at a college, but I got that message for myself. For a long time I felt by not going on and getting a Ph.D. and not going the route of being a professor, I was somehow less of a person. At St. Croix I was still struggling with that, not valuing what I was doing as much as I think it should be valued.

Now I can't even imagine myself thinking that there would be such a hierarchy. If anything, I keep feeling that I want to know more about younger children, and what's happening before I see them in high school class, and what is happening in the kindergarten and preschool. That seems to me equally as important as being a professor in a university.

Getting Lost in a Big School

When I came back to California and taught in a public high school, I learned that in a huge high school, a lot of kids were not used to having teachers talk with them individually. I ended up taking an individual interest in a lot of students, and in doing that I got the sense that this was unusual for them, or unusual for them to get encouragement in math.

I had been hired for my qualifications in teaching anything from remedial math to calculus and yet they wanted me to teach the low-level algebra courses and one geometry section. So I was teaching a lot of kids who really didn't want to be in my classroom; they didn't want to be taking math at all. Some of them felt that they couldn't do math, or that it was completely boring. I felt I had to make it interesting. That was a little frustrating at the beginning for me, because the kind of math course I was expected to teach was not intrinsically interesting to me.

I got around a lot of that by showing an individual, personal interest in the students, and also showing them I had confidence in their learning. I tried to stay away from a lot of the drill that they had been used to, even though it had a place in that class, and they did need some.

I followed up on students who were either having difficulty or were trying to isolate themselves completely and just not be part of the class. I had the sense that they had gotten away with this for a long time. It was unusual to have someone almost forcing them to be part of the group. On the whole I felt that in that situation I was encountering more discipline problems.

Also, suddenly there was a system for the bookkeeping, and the grade books, and attendance, and all of these things that I hadn't really had to conform to in my experience as a teacher before. There was so much general collecting of data on these students that it detracted from my teaching math and took up a lot of time. But if I had had to stay on there, I think I would have enjoyed it. There I could contribute a lot and learn a lot from faculty in other disciplines, especially some of the people in special education that I got to know a little bit.

I became attached to my students in that one semester, and interested in the problems in a big public school where some kids could really get lost in the shuffle. In a sense that's where I felt I might have been able to make a difference just keeping track of students and continuing to interact with them even if I weren't their teacher. This would include following up on some of the suggestions I had made to those I felt shouldn't have been in the remedial class, but should have been in the more advanced class.

Public vis-à-vis Private Schools

I felt much smaller in the public school. I was much more aware of the whole train of authority. I was here at the bottom, there's my department chair, there's the principal, and that principal is accountable to the state. The justification for everything I had to do could be put off on someone else: a principal could easily say, "Well, I have to do this for the state, it's part of our funding." It ended up being so removed from education. Somehow [in a private school] we are justified on a different level.

There seems to be some huge, monster bureaucracy overlying the whole public school system, something that made me feel less comfortable about being in a public school full time. I felt as if I made less of a difference, whereas in this private high school I notice differences on all sorts of levels, including policy decisions about how the school is run, or the content of the curriculum.

I've met some public school teachers through EQUALS that I think are fairly happy in their teaching, but a little envious of some of the things in my situation that make it easier. I know people who are teaching in public schools because they feel a strong commitment to public education and are willing to make some other sacrifices, to put up with some things or try to change them. I would have to have a sense that I could make a difference. Maybe that time will come.

In fact I do have a very strong commitment to public education, and partly that comes from my family. My father would never have considered sending us to private schools. When I asked him recently—given the state of some public schools—what he would do, he would definitely still send us to public school. Yet it seems there is a big quandary for individual teachers wanting to teach in a situation that is productive, and one in which they really can teach and not babysit.

Pressures from Parents

I would say parents are concerned about grades, not so much about the students' SAT scores or achievement scores. I don't think they see the link so closely with our classes and those scores. But they are really concerned about grades and in fact we are seeing this year how that might be influencing our enrollment in advanced science courses, a lot of courses that are known to be difficult.

There is a sense that some kids are avoiding these because of the chance that they might get a "B" instead of an "A" in the course. I don't really know what we are going to do about that, but something has to be done. There are some students who will take on any challenge regardless of the grade, which is not important to them. I would like to see more students doing that, and they might, if there weren't all this pressure to get into the right school for college. Among our students there is enormous pressure to go to certain schools.

It is important to the kids, how they measure up at home. I am not sure individual teachers can do a lot about this question, except to talk to kids about education and what's important. I am not sure how easy it is to re-educate parents to accept different reward systems. I don't see it as very easy.

Respect and Autonomy

One of the most important things for me here at University High is that I
feel my ideas about education are respected and I can act on them.* It is
important for teachers to have respect from their administrators and other
teachers; respect may be almost the top thing. They need to be good
teachers, trained well, but it seems that, to keep good teachers, we have to
show a lot of respect and allow a certain amount of autonomy.

There seems to be a balance between letting teachers teach exactly how and
what they want to teach (I am sure I would disagree with some things,
especially if I had children in those classes) and recognizing the need for
some guidelines. Yet it is important that teachers use their best judgment in
teaching. Support for professional development is important too. At this
school, we are expected to take courses and workshops, or attend
conferences, and we have the time and financial support to do that.

Within the math department we have been able to develop our courses the
way we want to, and we are supported by the administration. Somebody isn't
there telling me, "You are not doing this right; do it that way"; or "Teach
this subject." In the department we argue about things. We have different
points of view but we can reach some agreement and be flexible enough to
change. Among the faculty a certain amount of respect is shown across
disciplines, just in the way people interact and ask each other's advice.

Who Teaches What

The teachers in the department decide every year what we would like to
teach. Certain people have favorite courses they have developed, but there is
always a push to somehow stretch ourselves and make sure that someone
who has been teaching upper level courses for a couple of years gets to teach
a Math I course. It is partly a matter of the teacher's choosing it; the chair of
the department pushes us in that direction to make us branch out.

In public school when I came in as a temporary person, I was assigned
remedial math courses mostly, and a little geometry section. It was
understood that the senior person taught the precalculus class. A teacher just

---

*In 1990, University High School in San Francisco enrolled 385 students and had a
faculty of 60 people. Twenty-five percent of the students were minorities and 100%
of the students went on to four-year colleges. Nearly 20% of the students received
financial aid.

entering the school would not be allowed to teach calculus, no matter what her background was. It just seemed silly. I was allowed to teach calculus my first year here, as well as other courses.

Inadequacy, Responsibility, Maturity

I didn't get involved in the students' lives outside the classroom during my first year at the school where I am teaching now. I think it was because I was new. The students didn't know me, so I wouldn't be someone they would approach. Last year they did on a couple of occasions that were significant to me. I felt that dealing with a crisis in someone else's life, especially a student's, is something I don't have a lot of experience with, and not any training for.

I see students seeking me out more and more and I am more open about sharing my concerns. Students realize that I am interested, and concerned about them and that I am someone they could turn to. It seems important to me that they have someone they can talk to, because some of the things that come up are too big to confide in a peer. They need some adult help; that puts me in an interesting position, first feeling inadequate having not had this experience, and then feeling the responsibility.

In my first year of teaching as a Peace Corps volunteer, my students were almost my age; they were maybe a year younger than I was. I think all teachers go through a period of figuring out that they are in positions of responsibility, that they are adults and can act that way with their students. Some friends of mine have gone into teaching, and it is important to them to be sort of on the same level as their students. I know people who have started out that way and then realized, "My role is not to be a peer of these people I am teaching; what they really need from me is not that at all. What they need is much more, and is what they should get from an adult." That kind of awareness shows how things evolve for you in teaching.

Dealing with things that come up in the students' lives, I felt, on one hand, I was acting on a gut level of feeling very compassionate and empathetic towards the person in trouble, and then suddenly realizing that that wasn't enough of a role. I had to rise above this and see that these students were turning to me as someone who might be able to take action. Those occasions were turning points for me.

Students Learn to Ask Questions and Compose Problems

This year I've been able to do things in the classroom that were not purely mathematical, but more emphasizing the process of education, my contact, and my communication with my students. I'm having them think a lot about their responsibilities, themselves as teachers of each other and of themselves. Having them keep journals has helped as well.

I feel that most of my students tend to learn best when they are allowed to explore on their own before they are given information. In my teaching, sometimes I'll lead them very carefully through steps, but sometimes the process is open ended, having them develop ideas and not being told so much.

Especially in a math class, this way is important because otherwise it is so easy to present material. It's also easy for the students to learn mechanical devices and do quite well on that level, and not really learn mathematics. It's important to me to allow them to make discoveries on their own, to come up with questions. It is difficult to generate from students good questions that will stimulate their own learning, but gradually it happens.

When the students can come up with questions from their own curiosity, then they are so much more ready to listen or to find ways to answer their own questions. I see part of my role as a teacher as trying to make it work backwards, and having them come up with the questions. I can help them with the setting or provide a context where they can more easily see patterns or see relationships, or get a sense of how to attack some unfamiliar problems.

Most recently I've asked the students to put themselves in the place of the teacher and come up with good problems for other people. It was one explicit way of getting them to ask questions. In fact, I was doing this in the first week of classes as a review of material they had had in the previous year. It seemed to get them to realize that they could be part of the learning process.

I gave them a sheet of familiar topics from the previous year. They would come up with a verbal problem resulting in a quadratic equation or something involving a proof using coordinate geometry—something they would bring from their basic geometry class—or a problem about parallel perpendicular lines or intersections. The students could put their questions in different categories and work in pairs to solve other people's problems.

Journals, Analyses, and Critiques

This particular group of classes are keeping journals this year. One of my goals has been to vary the routine a bit, and to spend maybe fifteen minutes a day at least on writing. I decided I would bring in the journals every Thursday, so I would have a chance to read them at my leisure, and it would be a way for me to communicate with my students.

What I have seen so far of their writing has impressed me. I thought it could be very open ended on some days. This first time, I really wanted them to talk about the process of making up a problem and modifying someone else's problems. That made sense to them and I just love their insight. It is so worthwhile for me to read their journals, and it seems obvious from the writing that they get a lot out of it.

We got into analyzing each other's math problems, and that's partly what they talk about in their journals. They critiqued other problems in pairs. Before doing that, to give them a general sense of how we could critique a problem, I divided them into two larger groups of maybe six people each. I put a problem on the board that had been inspired by someone else's problem in the previous class. They had large-group discussions with a leader to keep them on track, and somebody recorded their discussion. They talked about what kinds of things they would have to change, or what would have been the intent of the person, and how they could write a problem that really got to the point.

A Sense of Participation

Working and learning together, as in the adult world, doesn't happen in the math classroom very much, but it could. A lot of things kids learn in a high school science or math class give them the feeling that this is stuff that somebody worked on way back then. We are just learning it again, reporting on it, but not involved in furthering it at all. I was struck by this in my first trip to Morocco because, even more there than anywhere else, I felt those students viewed their role as passive, receiving information, accustomed to a lecture format.

I wanted to help them get a sense of participation, a sense that they could actually help further the whole field of mathematics. It is hard to get that across to kids, and even to graduate students. There is a lot you can do, even at the high school level, working on data that people are collecting right now, analyzing data, and getting a sense that this is what people do, and this information has not fallen from the sky. Students need to have a sense that they are really participating.

Nonteachers in the Classroom

We have had people come in to talk to a science class or history class; in general I like the idea. There are a lot of people who could be excellent teachers who are not in teaching; to tap that resource is a wonderful idea. I don't know of any private schools that are using that kind of arrangement.

I can see some teachers thinking that the outside person is encroaching on their territory and doesn't have a background in education, and sort of resenting that; but it could be done in the right way, to maximize the contribution of the nonteachers. It would be good if you could pair that person with an experienced teacher.

I'm also thinking of people at the university, because of my father. He sometimes says that when he retires he will do some high school teaching. Being a teacher has always been an important part of his being a professor. I think he would be wonderful with that age group. I hope it happens.

The Search for Tomorrow's Teachers

A very few students ask me every so often about the possibility of becoming teachers. Their parents don't want them to be teachers. Some of the parents directly say, "We appreciate what you are doing as a teacher but we would not want our kids to be teachers." It is frightening. It always puts me in a bizarre position, where these parents obviously value education for their kids but they can tell me almost to my face that they don't want this for their kids. Yet they are relying on us as teachers to do a good job.

As a faculty we have talked about whether we as teachers, who are really interested in what we are doing, can do some public relations in the community among people who might not even consider teaching. I think some teachers respond to questions with a bit of an apology. Not really saying "I'm just a teacher," but in effect saying something similar. If we could show our enthusiasm for what we are doing and our feeling that we are doing something very important, that would be at least a small step.

Notes

[1] Also known as the Book of Changes, the *I Ching* is one of the Chinese five classics, a book of divination intended to provide guidance.

[2] Richard Douglas McCallum, "Developmental Constraints on the Comprehension of Main Ideas in Exposition," 1987. Thesis: Ph.D. in Education, University of California at Berkeley, May 1987.

[3] The Mentor Teacher Program is a California state-funded program designed to recognize excellent teachers and to encourage them to make their expertise available to their colleagues.

[4] For a good overview of Piaget, see Herbert Ginsburg and Sylvia Opper, *Piaget's Theory of Intellectual Development, An Introduction* (Englewood Cliffs, NJ: Prentice-Hall, Inc., 1969); and John L. Phillips, Jr., *The Origins of Intellect: Piaget's Theory* (San Francisco: W.H. Freeman and Co., 1969).

Part 4

THE POLITICS OF EDUCATION

Public education is one manifestation of public policy, and public policy is shaped through political activity. Politics can appear as a necessary evil, as the art of the possible, or the process of who gets what, when, where, and how.

The internal politics of education affects decisions about the structure and function of schools: for example, curriculum, instruction, assessment, and assignment of teachers and students to classes. School politics provides a way of dealing with conflicting demands. Teachers understand that the internal politics of the school site and district is not bounded by the playground's edge but is influenced by the larger demands of society.

The external politics of education is played out through public debate and elections that shape public policy, where schools fare badly. As a consequence, the confidence and security of teachers and students have suffered. When teachers observe the effect of political decisions on education, they feel sabotaged.

Sallyann Tomlin and Frank Gold understand the larger political context that affects school decisions. When decisions are adverse, they do not accept the role of victim. Instead, they push for reform in the face of obstacles and disinterest, showing their individuality, their vulnerability, and their determination.

Sallyann Tomlin

Frank Gold

Sallyann Tomlin:
Teacher as Future Principal

An Attraction to Political Activity

I went to school in Berkeley in the 50s. School was not hard, but I had to learn English. I spoke Chinese first at home, so my oral language has never been that strong. I've had some horrible teachers. I had a 7th grade and 8th grade English teacher who ridiculed me, and a horrible male geometry teacher who was the most uncompassionate person I've ever met. Just nasty. I've never gone out for things that would require me to do public speaking. That's been a real hurdle, because I'm going to have to start doing that when I'm a principal.

I got into journalism class in Berkeley High School, and from there became editor of *The Jacket*, which in those days was the school's daily newspaper. I had a very free schedule. Growing up in Berkeley in those days was fun. I had a lot of friends who were politically active; their parents were professors at Cal.

My parents did not want me to go to Cal because they thought it would be too overwhelming and too close to home. We were Presbyterian, and so they were looking at Presbyterian colleges. I didn't like Los Angeles, so Occidental was out. I ended up going to Lewis and Clark in Portland. It was great, and I enjoyed that experience thoroughly, although it was very White and very isolated. I was somewhat surprised by that but I didn't have a whole lot of ethnic consciousness in those days, and there were some foreign students. I majored in history and political science, with a minor in education.

I graduated from college in 1968, and took a year off and worked in politics. It was very easy in Oregon to get into politics; things are on a really localized level there. I worked for the county central committee of a political party and saw the campaign of '68. Then I decided to come back to California.

My dad died, my mom had never been employed before, and she decided to get her teaching credential. I moved back home and kind of watched her go through the process, and decided, "No, this is never going to be for me."

(laughs) Immediately, I went in the other direction, and I got into law school. I did one year of that, and absolutely hated it, although it was kind of a lark for me. I was attracted by the glamour of it all but discovered I really didn't enjoy it as much as I thought I would.

Hesitation, and Giving "Operation Fair Chance" a Try

After a lot of floundering around, I got my credential at Cal State Hayward through Operation Fair Chance, where my mom had done hers. At that point she had worn me down; I couldn't think of any more arguments against it. My hesitancy was that I was never very comfortable with children. I had done some camp counseling and not felt teaching was something I wanted to do. I thought I'd give teaching a year, and that this program would probably give me good exposure. I'd have a chance to get in there and see whether I liked it or not. If it had been a negative experience, I would have gotten out of it fast.

The program's thrust was that a teacher can learn best in the classroom, not through books, and not through a lot of courses. There was almost no classroom work. The program doesn't exist any more, and it was pretty besieged when I was there. The people in power said, "This is totally unacceptable. These people are not going to be good teachers. They're not learning anything."

We would spend four days a week as student teachers; one day a week we would get together and do sharing sessions and brainstorming and maybe math workshops and reading workshops. You know, "This is a sentence group. What do you do with a sentence group? This is how you make games," that sort of thing. It was wonderful. I didn't know how wonderful it was until I got out and realized what I had missed in a traditional preservice course, and of course, I hadn't missed anything.

My master teachers were a 4th grade teacher and a kindergarten teacher. They were outstanding. I lucked out, I really did. I could have gotten someone who was turned off and it would have changed the course of everything. As it turned out, these two women were good friends and were part of a group of women studying and practicing Piagetian education.

Support Group and Open Classroom

When I finished the program and got my credential in 1972, I was hired to teach 3rd grade at Highland Elementary, a traditional K–6 school in East

Oakland, where I had done my student teaching.* I immediately found myself a part of the group with built-in support right there.

I learned about factions on a school staff; I learned about support groups. There was definitely a group of people interested in making things happen at school: building playgrounds, raising funds, you know, doing extra things for kids.

At some point my concern got past just an interest in educational theory and became more of an interest in humanizing my classroom. I took several courses that synthesized all the different fads that were going on at the time, like the manipulatives, the open classroom, the Piagetian theories, and how you could set up your classroom to accommodate a lot of these things. It caused a lot of flak at the school, because we were the bunch with the plants and the sofas. People asked, "What's a 'learning center'?" and it was nice to have the theory to back it up. We would get together and say, "OK, we want to do more cooking in the classroom. Let's make all these individualized recipes." We would all work together and assembly-line the whole thing, and we would share everything. It was really a nice support group.

My second teaching position was at Hoover, a K–4 school, with open classrooms. Basically "open" meant there was a shared area: counters, wet-counters, cooking area, telephone, teachers' work space. It all opened onto the classrooms. You could be in a work area and you could see your classroom. There were no walls; everything was connected by ramps. The school was built in a circular style. You could see anybody who entered the building, and they could see you, although they might not be able to get to you immediately. The library was in the middle portion, so we could all look down into the library. There were partitions that were like hanging bulletin boards and you could move them. I have heard that all the bulletin boards are right next to each other now, forming a wall. (I understand selling the community on open classrooms was really difficult.)

We also didn't have desks. We had little moveable carts that we rolled around. The room was air-conditioned. It was pretty sterile, but nice and spanking clean. I learned to work with the people I didn't know before. You really have to be flexible and accommodating in many ways to work in that setup.

---

*In October 1990, the Oakland Unified School District enrolled 51,000 students and employed 2,700 teachers in 59 elementary, 16 intermediate, and 6 comprehensive high schools. The student demographics were: 57.3% African American; 18.3% Asian; 15% Hispanic; 8.8% White; and .5% Other. In Fall 1990, 52.1% of the families of Oakland students were receiving AFDC.

When we moved into our 4th grade pods we had a male teacher, a woman teacher who was pretty strong and set in her ways and in her style of teaching, a brand new first-year teacher, and me. There were many different styles and many different degrees of organizational ability. It really was fun, but the cliques among the grades developed. You know, "First grade is flaky, 4th grade always gets to go on the field trips," that kind of thing.

It worked well because we were all equals. We all had strengths, we all had weaknesses, and we were all exposed. You just don't have that intimidation, that insecurity, because either you all swim or you all sink. I think that was a good lesson. We had to respect each other and we could benefit each other. More than anything else I think it was the physical plant that helped. We were physically exposed, and the principal gave us a lot of latitude.

Moving Toward Professionalism

My growth as a teacher started with picking out teachers that I would like to emulate, from little, specific ideas that I would like to try in my classroom, to programs, units of study, to philosophy. For a while, our group was having weekly chats. We would meet at someone's house and just chat. Anything was up for grabs. Courses: "Where do I find these materials? Is there a course that I can do? What are you doing this summer?" Anything. It was just a support group, and then from there, "How do I incorporate all these things? How do I make them happen right now?"

Lesson design is valuable for a new teacher, just to make sure that she's covering all the bases. I think that it's good to be aware, to have it in your consciousness so that you do know that you're not just doing things automatically or subconsciously. Also it's interesting.

My principal will go into a classroom and say, "Do you have time to come in and script-tape me?" Basically to script-tape means to write down everything that the person says, and then have a post-conference and talk about all the elements that came out. Script-taping works better than simply taping, because you can see body English, and you can see reactions.

It depends what the person wants. If a teacher is having trouble with a group of kids in her class, one of the results might be, "Well, I noticed that in the course of this lesson you were never really over in that area of the room. Why don't you try standing over there, putting your hand on the kid's chair?" Being there really helps. "I noticed that your lights weren't turned on." Maybe that kind of thing, and having people, like my principal, open enough to say, "Would you mind coming in to watch me do this lesson?" It's really exciting. He is interested in growth and he is interested in what I have to say. It's at a level that's so professional. That's one thing about jargon; it is a common terminology.

Styles of Help: Competence and Friendship

Good relationships between teachers can occur on two levels, and I've experienced both. One is working with a teacher who is completely competent, who knows the material, has resources, and is somebody that you can depend on to help you out. "I need some exciting spelling ideas. My kids hate spelling. What can I do? How do I jazz this up?" Those kinds of things, where the teacher is serving as a resource.

On the other level, teachers are good friends. They may not be the ones you would pick as your teacher of the year, but they are good friends. They're good people, they give you emotional support, and they give you psychological support, which is also something that is really necessary. I've been in both situations. I have some close friends who probably aren't terrific teachers, they're OK teachers, but that's not what we're bringing into the relationship.

Getting help like new spelling ideas is not very easy. Usually you approach an older teacher, and she brings you under her wing. Then when it's time for you to get out from under her wing it might be a little bit hard. (laughs)

Student Leadership and Behavior

As far as discipline is concerned, this works for any age from little kids through high school: I've done time out, lots of class meetings from the very start with the whole class, just peer kinds of things. That's really helpful, to let them run the class meetings. I do it in a simple format, where up on the chalkboard there is the agenda. It says, "Problems, Concerns, Plans, and Sharing." Kids have an option of signing up, so that they're categorizing what they want to say during the class meeting. That really helps. A lot of things get talked out.

It helps to do class meetings right after the long morning recess when everybody is out there beating each other up. It's student directed. It gets me away from being the big disciplinarian, and it gets them acting a little more responsible.

To keep it from dragging on, there are usually three numbers below each topic so you might have at most twelve people talking. Sometimes it's a very short meeting. With this method, I see much less need for individual contracts for behavior. I see a lot of peer interaction. I see kids with leadership qualities emerge, which is an interesting side effect that goes with the process.

Talking with Parents

I start articulating to parents why I'm doing what I do in the classroom when everything is well under control. I tell them when I feel comfortable with the program and see it working, and can point to specifics: "This is what happened with your child. Remember last year when you said that this was happening? Look at this; this is another way to attack the problem." That is a beginning in parent contact.

It is satisfying to be able to do that. At Hoover, with the constant exposure, it was something that we had to develop in a hurry. We had to sit down to parent conferences. The principal was great. He said, "What's this with the report cards? Let's do it through parent conferences." So we would forego the paperwork and sit down and have conferences. That gets your technique going fast.

At Highland School in 1972, the student majority was Black. Anything you did above the minimum was really well received. The principal was a nice lady, a good person who loved to give verbal support. She was not really affirmative in stating what her programs were, what she believed in. I didn't get a sense of her philosophy other than, "Let's be nice to the children."

Parents' involvement in the school was just token. One parent would sign all the documents for the school. When I moved to Hoover, it was a little bit more of the same. The craziness was still there. There were a lot of incidents with parents. There were a lot of really frustrated people who did not have anywhere to dump and would find that the school was the most accessible place. That was hard.

The Road Toward Administration

I was at Glenview [in Oakland], a very small school with 12 teachers but it really got me going in the direction of administration. When I was project facilitator—the job has now been eliminated—I supported the teachers with all the budgetary things, all the supplies, the ordering, that kind of thing. I served on all the school site committees for the state and federal programs. I did the discipline for the school, so we worked on smoothing out the policies that were inconsistent here and there. I was the first step at the office. When the kids were finally sent to the office, I would see them first so that Bob, the principal, could be the "ultimate." I would take over the classroom whenever it was needed. I did that quite a bit.

As far as curriculum was concerned, it was a unique situation, because the teachers were used to having closed doors. They talked about their "teaching charisma." "My kids are successful because of my teaching charisma." Therefore, all kinds of things can be implied from that: discipline policies don't have to be consistent; curriculum standards don't have to be consistent; record-keeping doesn't have to be completed.

Every once in a while the younger teachers would say, "I'm really in a jam. What's going on here? Could you come in and model this for me?" That was great. It was really nice to be asked, but it takes a long time to build up that trust with the staff, especially when they've been there a long time. You're the new kid on the block, and you're actually younger than they are.

Released Time for Teachers: Chances for Growth

If I were a principal, I would work to make the opportunities for growth available, with lots of released time for teachers who want to learn more. Some don't want it. Some teachers think that their classes will not survive if they leave for a day. That's OK.

Our cluster is doing a whole new timetable thing. Every school in the cluster will start at 8:30. The whole idea is to mandate cluster minimum days. On those minimum days, you'll have a menu, you'll get to choose which school you go to. Do you want one in cooperative learning? Do you want one in writing? You go to that school. That's one way of creating released time. As it is now, we get five days a year and this will add even more, I think. I haven't exhausted the possibilities of staff development. It's got to be something where the staff either designs it, or has a great deal of input. Otherwise, it's just meaningless.

The principal does not have a great deal of discretion about inservice training and staff development, not as much as is needed. My ideal school would have released time for team-building too, so that the teachers can monitor their own programs, see where they are, and coach each other so that the principal doesn't have to be the big, bad guy.

There's never enough time for meetings, and there's probably not all that much flexibility in the system, when you get right down to it. We have certain required numbers of days and hours and not a whole lot of latitude, but you could have teachers taking over each other's classes—that's a good way to do it—or a principal, or a curriculum assistant, doing that.

The View From the Principal's Office

I have experienced a loss of energy as a teacher in the past. In this case, it was because of a very domineering kind of principal. He was basically Attila the Hun for many years, and would browbeat the staff. As a teacher you don't speak up; you just don't. You don't make waves, but in the school where a friend of mine is principal, he is beginning to make a difference.

His style is different. It would be different from mine. He's very reserved; in appearance, he's very straight, just unbending, although he is not that way with me because we've been friends for so long. He's not a partying type, and that has kind of put him two steps behind, because he's not one of the gang. He probably could never be one of the gang, but as principal he is putting more energy into that school.

The elementary school principal has a good chance to make an impact. There's a lot of stuff that comes down from the district, but for the most part you can remove yourself from it. I also see the principal's office as a stepping stone. Right now I'm not willing to give up the school setting. I like the contact with the kids; it's a combination of the best of things for me. It gives me a chance to work on leadership and executive kinds of abilities and organizational kinds of things. I love to organize. I love to sit there and figure out systems and see from an overall point of view.

I've learned a lot about the way a school needs to run. It's something that never even occurred to me, except to complain about it when I was a teacher. Classroom teachers are really isolated, but the school principal has a chance to see something through. There's a plan there. Three years, five years, and it's a neat feeling to be able to see something that you're molding.

Administrator as a Help to Teachers

I think that teachers deserve a chance to be the best that they can be in a nurturing environment, and they can't do that if they're fighting an administrator all the time. Hopefully I won't forget—when I become an administrator—what it takes to become a teacher. If some forget, maybe they weren't that good to begin with as teachers.

I think that you used to be able to be a principal without having been a classroom teacher. After the war—this is just rumor because I'm not that old—I heard that they pulled men into school off the streets. These were P.E. coaches and assorted hangers-on, and they made them all principals. Now those are the people who are starting to retire and it's creating a lot of openings for principals. Those guys are all taking the golden handshake.

Representation of women as principals is a little bit better at the elementary school level but certainly not in upper management. There are very few women superintendents right now. And what is it, one or two state superintendents? At that level I have to wonder how much educator you have to be and how much politician you need to be.

Parent as Client

If I were a principal, I would organize a school the same way that I organize my classroom. One of my big priorities is giving choices. Students need to have choices; teachers need choices too; and I think parents need choices. Parents are our clients. There's no way that we should be able to ram down one style of education just because they don't happen to be involved or know better.

My ideal staff would have teachers with choices of style, with different styles that play to their strengths. You know, open education is not for everyone and there are varying degrees of it. Some people are much more comfortable in a more structured classroom. In the ideal situation, parents would know their kids well enough to say, "This teacher suits my child's learning style better."

I have one child. He's six, and he goes to Joaquin Miller School in Montclair [Oakland]. He's probably the only child who has ever requested a transfer away from a suburban school. "Surely you mean the other way around, don't you, lady?" My husband's Black, an attorney. We looked at the Orinda schools and the Moraga schools, and felt that program for program he would get as much in a more integrated school in Oakland. That is our feeling for right now.

I'm generally pleased with what's happening, and I'm sure that his social growth is being taken care of up there. Past the 3rd grade, I'm not going to predict. I really believe in public schools, and I want to continue believing in the public schools, so I really don't want to have to put him into something elite.

Public Awareness and Teacher Morale

I think teachers perceive the public as not understanding what they're all about. Part of putting forth the worthwhileness of education is selling it to businesses, selling it to industry, because someone's going to have to take up some slack. I do favor school-industry partnerships.

To get the public more informed, teachers, and education as a whole, need to stop getting such bad press. It's one of those situations where all of the negative gets printed: all the lawsuits, all the battery, and all that stuff. The good stuff never really does get printed, and there is plenty of good stuff. You see, that's part of the problem with teacher morale. It's like what happens when the principal comes into my room once a year and immediately says, "You're not following the lesson plan," and doesn't say anything about all the other neat things I've been doing all year long.

The NEA did some PR, some short spots on TV. I don't think the message was clear that those were real teachers. I didn't believe they were real teachers. When you see them for 30 seconds and they're out there with a platitude, it's just not convincing. I do know they were real teachers because we were asked to audition for those dumb things. It wasn't an appealing idea to me. Probably something more in depth would have been. It's so hard to capsulize and at the same time present something that everyone can relate to.

Someone said teachers are complacent. I don't know whether "complacent" is the right word for teachers, but they're certainly conservative. They're afraid to make statements; they're afraid to lobby. I understand the historical background, and I understand that they're trying to come off as professionals, but in order to get the clout we're going to have to get past that stigma.

I think teachers are afraid of the union label. They would prefer to call themselves members of "professional organizations," trying to get away from the blue-collar thing. I really think that if teachers are going to strike, they need to make it an effective strike. An effective strike is labor backed. In Oakland we strike every three years. Recently, the strikes have been effective. That's the part of being a principal that I don't relish.

Frank Gold:
Teachers, Jobs, Politics, and the Public

Knowing that a Teacher is Something

I came from Chicago, lived right in the city in a working-class neighborhood. We were a Jewish family; not religious, but still Jewish. Education and teaching were highly valued, so a teacher was something. The first of my dad's family who got through college became a teacher, and that was considered the greatest thing in the world. Now nobody goes into teaching, because it's not good enough any more.

I entered high school in February of 1956. The Chicago schools were heavily segregated; *Brown v. Board of Education* had come down in '54 but hadn't really been implemented.[1] The school district was allowing students to ask for voluntary transfers from one school to another. You'd say, "I want to go to Austin High instead of Marshall High because I want to take Latin. Marshall doesn't have Latin." They'd say, "OK." Austin is all White; Marshall's all Black. They stopped that with my entering class.

Marshall High School went from probably 90 per cent Black to 50–60 per cent Black overnight, literally overnight. All they had wanted for these Black kids—the really good ones—was to work at the post office. They didn't have physics, they didn't have chemistry; and the school had 2–3,000 kids at the time. There was nothing in the way of academic expectations. Even so, it turned out to be a good experience for me.

Two Math Teachers

I had a math teacher in high school, Gloria Cantierri, who was very good. I look back at her now and I realize what it was. It's the same thing kids always tell me, "She's a good teacher because she cares." That's what she did. She cared.

Annie Rollefson was my teacher when I took first year algebra and I did all right. I took geometry and I did pretty well, you know, B stuff. I was kind of a bright kid and I was bored, precocious, and troublesome from time to time. I didn't care that much for school but I liked being there. Then I got her for advanced algebra, and I couldn't do it. That semester was just terrible. Annie Rollefson was just getting ready to retire, a little short lady walking around with a meter stick that came up to her chin. She pounded it. I was terrified of her. We were all terrified of her, all 35 kids in the class. One day she called me out in the hall, grabbed me by the shirt, looked up at me—and I'm not tall—and she said, "Gold, you just don't have it. I don't ever want to see you in another math class." I was thrilled to get through that course with a D.

Terror at the Blackboard

We used to go to the board in that class, probably about a third or half the class, draw our lines, put our names at the top, and then kind of move our shoulders so we'd have a space. Then she'd give a problem and we'd all work it. You couldn't move your head left or right to look to see. I didn't want to see what Eldon Stanek or Don Midid was doing, because she'd be behind you with that meter stick.

The one that was the killer was the quadratic formula. She had us write it on top of our little space, and she said, "Derive the quadratic formula." I didn't know what was going on. I couldn't do it. There's Don; he's doing it. Don went to MIT [Massachusetts Institute of Technology]. Eldon Stanek, he's doing it. He went to IIT [Illinois Institute of Technology]. I had no clue. If you didn't get it the first day, you had to come back the next day. This would go on. So I'm up there with the next batch of kids, and I still can't do it. Finally, I memorize it from the textbook, but I have a terrible memory and so I get stuck about halfway through. I never learned how to do completing the square, so it made no sense to me.

Before this experience, I thought I could do most anything. I didn't have any particular talent like my father, who was artistic. Math was something that I wanted to do, but I just couldn't do it. Then, next semester, I got into a class with Gloria Cantierri, and I went right to a B. Here was a person who did not humiliate; there were no putdowns in the class. She went on the assumption that, if you were there, you could do it. Maybe you didn't get it the first time, that was OK. I find myself relaying the same ideas to my students. I mean, who gets this the first time?

Honors Program and Coaching

I took a summer program between junior and senior year, kind of an honors program. She encouraged me to do it. I repeated advanced algebra and then I did the trig, which I took later again in the fall, so it was very easy.

The guy who ran the course had a different student present the lesson each day. There was time built in where he would sit down with you and take a look at what you wanted to do, and help determine a decent assignment. We had to do the assignment and answer questions. That was really scary stuff, and we were all graded by the class on how well we did it. It turned out that was fun, and an interesting approach. The next year I had a good solid math background, and was very successful as a senior.

Remember I was in a school that was in a major transition; they wanted to do things to help the most capable kids, because they knew the program fell short. They set up a program they called "coaching" in English, social studies, and math. It was an extra period in the day, and we did about six weeks with one subject, six with another. In addition, they taught us test-taking skills, which none of us had. The result was that we had a large number of Illinois State Scholarships out of this group, and we had six Merit Scholar finalists out of this little ghetto school at mid-year. We don't get that much out at Tam High.* It was really quite amazing. I realize of course that it was this kind of coaching, a real faculty effort.

I got an Illinois State Scholarship that I didn't use, but I felt good. It was good for the old self-esteem. I went to a small liberal arts college in Wisconsin. It was part of my parents' notion of introducing me to the middle class. It was one of the first times I encountered anti-Semitism.

Teaching Math and Learning a Repertoire

I took a math degree because I liked math, but I didn't want to be a mathematician; I wasn't that strong in it. I thought about teaching, and I took a class from a guy who talked about different styles of teaching. For

---

*Tam High, where Frank Gold teaches, is part of the Tamalpais Union High School District in Marin County. The district comprises 3 comprehensive high schools and 2 continuation/ opportunity high schools. The total student enrollment in the five high schools in October 1990 was 2,734 students and 148 teachers. The student demographics for the district were: 5% African American; 3% Asian; 86% White; and 6% Other. The percentage of families receiving AFDC in 1990 in the Tam High District was 4.4%.

about two weeks he did each lecture with a completely different style. He had some kind of "discovery" stuff; he had a very didactic lecture; he did a kind of stimulus-response involvement, non-directed; and a Socratic approach. I thought that was interesting because that's problem solving to me. You have to have a repertoire. Most people I'd encountered in teaching had no visible repertoire; they just had a methodology and they used it all the time.

I figured, OK, I needed to do something to make a living. The University of Wisconsin had a good internship program for teachers. I applied and they arranged for me to do an internship 20 miles from where my wife and I were living. I took three classes at the University, and then a semester entirely immersed in the school. About once a month someone from the University came in and observed. I thought that internship program was dynamite; it gave me a lot of respect for teaching.

The day before school started I met the woman who was supervising me. She was a department head and we were in a new wing. The building had just been completed; we moved in and everything was in a state of disarray. On the first day of school she had an operation and missed the first two weeks. When she came back, she came in and sat down in the back of my classroom, with papers in front of her—she was going to do some work. She watched me open a lesson in geometry and after maybe 10 minutes she got up, took all her stuff, and walked out. I don't think she ever came into another class of mine. I asked her about it, and she said, "I can see that you are going to be successful." I knew within the first week that it was something that I liked doing and that it was something that I could do. All the problems that I had anticipated weren't developing.

I entered teaching in the most exciting decade, I think, imaginable. Here I was with an expensive liberal arts college background in 1963 and I was going into education. Today people would say, "Why are you wasting your education by going into teaching?" That didn't occur; there was a notion of making a social contribution. To this day, I don't know how I could make a better social contribution than teaching.

Demonstration Project: Inductive Math

In my first year at Tam High, 24 years ago, we implemented a little project called Inductive Math. I was pulled from my classes, about three-quarters of the way through the school year, along with two other guys. One of them was the department chair and the other was Joe Gutierrez. It was basically discovery teaching. The way we filled the class was to take the freshman kids who really had math problems. It was an ideal situation for learning the craft of teaching.

There would be two of us in the class with 25 kids, team-teaching. We could do anything we wanted. We were able to design a portable classroom for the campus with little offices and storage rooms. The administrators just said, "Design it the way you want it," and it was built. It was carpeted, air-conditioned, and we had all the materials we needed. We had a budget, and we had an instructional aide who could do clerical stuff. The only thing we didn't have was a curriculum. We had no content, just a philosophy. We knew if you presented an interesting problem to the kids, and it wasn't remediation, the kids would go for it and a teacher who knows a lot of mathematics could follow through.

Joe and I warmed to this. The other guy tried, but he was older, a good teacher, but he didn't have this kind of flexibility and he didn't quite see the excitement of it. We had a great time because Joe and I would be in the room together. One of us would start; we might pick a problem like: "I'm thinking of a number from 1 to 16. What's my number?" Then we would go from there. The kids would always have impulsive answers, and then we would change the problem and say: "What's the minimum number of questions you have to ask?" Then we'd get into anything that was related to a binary system or a base two system and we would just go on. I would do something with the kids, and then Joe would see something from the back of the room, and he'd come in. It was interchangeable. One or the other. The kids were completely used to this. No problem for the kids at all. What it meant was these two energetic guys in their twenties, who had pretty good math backgrounds, could outrun 25 kids who were truly energetic and had miserable math backgrounds.

In those days, when you were not a really experienced person, you relied on speed. We had the stamina and the energy. We would come down on Sunday afternoons—Joe lived in Berkeley and I lived over here in Marin County—and we'd sit down in the classroom and figure out what we were going to do, where it might go, and what were all the possible branches. That was great.

Planning and Peer Coaching

We learned that we had to be a lot more accepting of these kids. It was a profound experience working with very poor math students in a nurturing setting. We would have the instructional aide sit in the back of the room and take notes. That way we would keep a record of what we did in each of these classes. The classes were anywhere from a double period to a period and a half; we never did it in one period. We didn't give these kids breaks or anything, we just sat there and did math, steady. We would talk about our teaching, and Joe would say, "When you did this, did you think about doing that?" Or "Did you notice how, when Earl Ray said something, you put him down?"

We began to develop what they now call "peer coaching." We developed not only our questioning skills but a whole relationship to kids. These kids were rough; we were breaking up fights all the time, but it was a great way to learn the craft. Whatever we learned in the way of techniques and insights that worked with these kids would certainly improve our work in our other classes. And it did.

Learning Acceptance and Modifying a Strategy

Earlier, Tam High used to have a program with one year of math required. The students who came out of that program could go into a two-year algebra course. In past years the school might get four or five kids who would even try it. In our Inductive Math course we had between 50 and 60—after just one quarter of the year—who were ready to try it. That pattern went on the next year, so 75 percent of these kids went on in mathematics, kids who before this program would have had only one year of mathematics during their whole high school career.

That meant that we had to beef up an entire program. It also meant that we lost kids like crazy. They would start the algebra course and they wouldn't succeed; the style of teaching was so different, and we weren't doing a good enough job on basic skills. So we adopted a modified strategy in Inductive Math where we started out the same way and instead of carefully avoiding fractions, for instance, we would begin throwing them in after the kids had security with dealing with algebraic constants.

We would have them solving equations and doing all kinds of great stuff, but with whole numbers or integers [that include negative numbers]. Then we would begin to build the frustration. About a third of the way through the school year, they would start saying, "I don't know how to add fractions. I want to learn to do this." Then we would carve out a day or two and sit down and get those old basic math books out and go through them with these kids. They'd love it. It was what they wanted to do. We would wait until they would start demanding it. At first we would reject it, "No, no." We thought we were clever.

We were getting a couple of years' growth in a year, and spending no more than half the year on what the test was measuring. We were very pleased by it, and it began to carry over in our other courses. The teaching in those classes really improved. Over a few years about half the department taught Inductive Math and we were stronger for it.

Of course, the funding ended. We did manage to get the Board of Education to adopt a reduced class size policy for these classes. At one time it was 13 kids to one teacher. It's still in effect in the contract; when the union became a bargaining agent in '76 we negotiated it right into the contract. So I think our ratio now in these classes is 18 to one. We still called it Inductive Math, but it was one period like everything else. We tended to be the same positive people teaching it, so we kept control of it that way. We did very much the same activities for at least a decade. We encouraged the kids to go on. We did a better job of giving them some of the skills that they needed, and we increased the ability to get out of the tracking system.

We're just now coming out of a period when a lot of these math classes were being farmed out to people who weren't math teachers. They can't teach this kind of stuff. So we went back to textbooks, traditional kinds of things. There was a new wave of textbooks, though, that were better. We helped these people as much as we could. I had a little bit of released time and money and did a lot of inservice with these [crossover] P.E. teachers or drafting teachers, whatever they were, who were teaching math. We seized control again, districtwide, and we said, "No. We've got to do a better job."

About two or three years ago we redesigned these math courses again away from remediation. They had been locked into meeting the minimum competency requirements. We've revised the courses entirely and had the math teachers teach it. We do things like experiential geometry, problem-solving, for the first two years. This is a three-year program; everybody takes three years of math, and we have had that before it was required by the board. We have been getting kids to take three years of math when the board was still requiring one, but we are now back to crossover teachers teaching these math courses.

Trying to Catch Them Doing Something Good

I've evolved. My teaching style is a lot different now from what it was. It used to be a high-energy kind of thing. Beginning teachers, even the best of them, aren't really very good because they don't have the wisdom that the experienced teacher can pick up. I can just do without any movement what I used to have to race around the room to do. I'm not sure how it happens; a lot of it is intuitive.

There was a time if a kid was having problems, I would say something. I would do the usual thing. I didn't do a lot of shouting like some people do, but I would stop and call attention to what he was doing, tell him to stop, or even be sarcastic. I used to be sarcastic. There was a kind of humiliation that went with that, and I wasn't aware of it at the time. I was just being clever. I was also younger and when you're younger you're closer to the kids. Now I don't do that. If I see a kid doing something I don't like, I just kind of carry on with what I'm doing, walk over and stand next to the kid. Presence alone usually takes care of it.

I don't have discipline problems in general because I don't confront kids, I don't humiliate kids, and I've learned a lot. This has evolved into my current style. It's more than avoiding confrontation; it's about getting in there and trying to catch them doing something good, and treating kids differently rather than trying to be equal. People come in to observe my class and they look for this kind of thing: "I noticed you didn't have any trouble with Ross. Ross is terrible in my class." You know, the things that they say to Ross sometimes—you understand. I'm not looking for trouble. I'm not looking for the kids to do badly. If they're in the class, I expect them to do the work just like Gloria Cantierri expected that I could do the work way back when.

A Union Background

I was from a union family. My father was a commercial artist, and there was no union for commercial artists. He wanted to do some organizing. I remember at one point he went to the painters' union—he figured it was close—and tried to get them to organize some of the studios where commercial artists worked. It was a lousy job situation for them. The work's seasonal, so they'd get laid off. They'd work six months and then not have anything for the other six months. He got into some kind of problem there, he had gotten blacklisted, and it became hard for him to get any decent jobs.

My mom was a secretary, active in community politics. They were both activists, very progressive people. It was not a good time when I was young, in the 50s, because the FBI was on our case all the time—used to call at all hours of the night, harassing us. My mother worked as a secretary for Pete Seeger for a while. I used to listen to Paul Robeson. So there was always a radical tradition in the family. It made perfectly good sense to be in a union.

Joining the CTA in Glendale

In my first teaching job, in Glendale, California, they had a teachers association. The assistant principal signed me up the first week of school; that was standard for the CTA. You got signed up so the school could get a 100 percent certificate. They used to give out these certificates that said, "100 percent Membership in the California Teachers Association." I signed up because I figured that was the thing to do, and there was nothing else.

Next year, an AFT [American Federation of Teachers] local formed in the standard way that I think AFT developed in California: there were five guys, known members, who had all been past presidents of the Glendale Teachers Association. They called themselves "commissioners" so there wouldn't be a hierarchy and they put out the Green Sheet. Now, the Green Sheet came out all over California. (I don't know if they always used green). It was the newsletter. They would raise issues about expenditures and money, how decisions were made, mistreatment of people. I'll tell you, in Glendale, a conservative place, when the Green Sheet appeared, everybody read it and talked about it. That was the only time anyone talked about any real ideas there.

There was a little interest in the AFT. There was also a big case in Pasadena about some guy in night school getting fired because he had a beard. The association didn't do anything, but the Pasadena Federation of Teachers did, and we read about it in the paper. Well, it turned out that the teacher who went in and was the advocate for the guy who got fired, was the one who became president of the California Federation of Teachers for 20 years, and is one of my major mentors, although I didn't know him then.

When I came to Tam High School, I joined the association, and I was building rep. The CTA is a professional association. The AFT is a labor union. I should go back and explain the difference. Accountants have professional associations, architects have associations, and this was an independent association. The NEA has state affiliates. The CTA, a state organization, is an affiliate of NEA. They were not in favor of any of the things that the union stood for.

Connections in the community are important to the AFT. We belong to all the labor councils. The association had nothing to do with any affiliations with labor. "Teachers are better than working people." All right? It's a really elitist thing. The association's organization was run by school management. They didn't believe in strikes. They didn't believe in radical action. They didn't believe in collective bargaining.

Some AFT History

The AFT was started in 1916 by women elementary school teachers in Chicago, some of the most powerful radical women in America. They built a mass movement among Chicago teachers. They were elementary, female teachers, just the opposite of what most people think of as the teachers' union in America. They threatened the dominance of the NEA nationally. They had a major supporter in John Dewey, who held AFT card #1. At one point, they surpassed the NEA in membership nationwide.

At about the time of World War I, there was a change. The administrators saw what was happening. They seized control of the NEA, and the AFT ran into problems. A lot of it was around politics, red-baiting, and so on at the time. The AFT was greatly diminished, but the movement came back in the 60s. There were a lot of people drawn into teaching who were different from people connected to teaching before. We brought a lot of these people into our union activities. The 60s saw an enormous growth of the AFT, nationwide. Not all of it was that progressive, but it was very progressive in California. We were heavily involved with the peace movement, we were heavily involved with supporting farmworkers. A lot of our people were involved in the support of Angela Davis. My local was the first local to pass a resolution supporting Angela Davis when she was right here in Marin County jail.

We were pushing collective bargaining because that was the way teachers and their employers could be made equal. I fell into this about a year or two after I came here because I got involved as a building representative while I was in the CTA. I remember we were negotiating salaries. After weeks or months it came down to one meeting where a team of four or five went in and the rest of us officers were waiting outside. They came out and said, "We have 24 hours to accept this offer or they adopt the same salary schedule."

I said, "If we can get a flyer out to the teachers we could get some organization, and we'll hit them at the next board meeting. They can't just do that." To a person, including the president of the association, they responded, "Ah, teachers won't do anything." I couldn't believe that, because people were doing things all around us. This was 1968—1968 was a big year—and these guys were just going to roll over.

Joining the AFT and Pushing Collective Bargaining

The next year I got back and there was a Green Sheet—sometimes it was blue here—and these people had formed an AFT local. I didn't even know most of the names; I had been here only a little while, but I went to one of the meetings, and I joined. There were about a dozen people. You needed about ten to get a charter, and I don't even know if they had the charter yet, but they formed a local and pretended they did. I immediately got put on the negotiating team.

We operated under the Winton Act, so you didn't have collective bargaining. It was a kind of "meet and confer" thing, but it was proportional membership. We had just enough to get more than half of one seat, so we got a full seat on this council, and I was the one. A couple of years later I got elected president.

We were trying to educate people about what collective bargaining was. We were taking all these militant stands that were drawing some people in and putting all these other people out. When I became president it was clear that we had confrontational things that were not necessary and certainly were not beneficial. We began to clean that up a little bit, and focus not on other teachers, and not on personal attacks on administration, but on principled attacks on policy.

At that time the AFT and the CTA could coexist in one school, but they had this thing called "negotiating councils," passed by the legislature, in an attempt by the CTA to avoid collective bargaining. Because it was proportional representation, in some school districts the counselors had a group or the coaches had a group, and if they had enough members they could get a seat. We used that as an organizing device. First we had one seat then we went to two seats. I was in there trying to sign up people from the other side at council meetings. It wasn't until 1976 that collective bargaining came to California, through statute. The AFT was pushing all this time. Until 1972, the CTA's official position was opposed to collective bargaining.

Drafting a Contract

So our union grew. It began educating people as to what a contract was. Get something from New York City, right? They had contracts in New York, they had contracts in Chicago, we could have contracts. There it was right in the contract: "If there's a violation of this, then here's how it gets resolved." It was a powerful idea to people who never had any sense of equality or redress.

I remember one day, maybe 1969, two other guys and I—it was a lot of men at this time—took a day off and we went over to my parents' apartment. (They had moved out from Chicago. That's what happens, you move 2,000 miles away and it's OK. But then, have a kid, and they're out here.) I had gotten them an apartment in Mill Valley here, so we went over to their apartment, sat down with all the contracts that we could gather, and we wrote a contract for the Tam High School District by lifting bits and pieces and throwing in the stuff that we wanted.

We had all kinds of nice stuff like class size and salary and decision-making, it was great. Then we put it out, and we educated people about this, and they began thinking. Our membership grew, and we got up to about a third of the teachers belonging to the AFT. We probably had more of the young ones.

The percentage of teachers who don't belong to either of the unions in the district varies; right now it's kind of high. At one time, it was certainly less than 10 percent, now it's maybe as high as 20–25 percent. But when the collective bargaining law passed, we had the first election in the history of California under this law, and we won. It surprised everybody, knocked CTA on its ass completely. We won with a third of the teachers as members. We had shown them that we could negotiate. We knew what it was about because we had taught the teachers what it was. So they picked us. We went in and negotiated a pretty good contract.

Views on a Strong Union

Having a strong union can lead to a kind of security for all parties involved, including the administration and the board of trustees. Agreements are made and people commit themselves to doing what they said they would do, and use procedures that no longer become arbitrary or haphazard. It's very important to know that, as a teacher, my work will be evaluated in such and such a way. The administration knows what it will do. It knows how we're going to resolve conflicts because we build those in. If there is a problem, we know what will happen next. We don't have to worry about conflicts necessarily becoming major obstacles.

I've always been proud that the AFT has a very good track record negotiating educational issues like smaller class sizes, like involving professional people and making professional decisions. In the 1960s, with one or two exceptions, it took a progressive position regarding parent involvement in schools and women's issues. AFT leaders statewide were women, so we did a lot so that women could have some decent security if they left to have children. They had benefits that they were entitled to. All this tends to be a stabilizing force in a school district. In the long run, in exchange for giving up their prerogatives for arbitrary behavior, the employers did get a sense of stability, and a lot fewer job actions.

Jobs, Due Process, and the Way Teachers Work Best

You don't find the word "tenure" in the California Education Code. There are two types of status for teachers as employees: one is probationary and the other is permanent. The distinction in terms has to do with dismissal procedures that change from time to time. For the first two years in California you don't have a right to due process; after that, you do. That's what tenure means in the public schools. Before we had these kinds of legislative protections, people were fired on the spot, fired for whatever reasons. AFT teachers were found out in the valley some place beaten up at the roadside. You went into a school board meeting, a public meeting, disagreed with some position they were taking, and you got fired. What tenure means to me is that you can't arbitrarily say to a person, "You're fired." You must establish cause and be able to substantiate the cause.

Teachers cannot function, do their jobs in the classroom, if they're looking over their shoulders all the time. There must be some due process. Any teacher who is not competent and has been teaching for four or five years has been declared competent by some school administration; otherwise, that person would have been dismissed earlier.

The leadership in some schools is in many ways less competent at dealing with teachers who need help than these teachers are in dealing with kids. That's unfortunate. There aren't that many teachers who are not competent. There are people who are assigned by administration to do things for which they're not prepared—like the hundreds of math teachers who are not prepared to teach mathematics but are assigned to mathematics. I don't need tenure. Never have. My union has never needed tenure. The key is due process. I don't know of any teacher who wants to work in a classroom next to a person who's not competent. It means my work is harder; I don't want that. So I'm in favor of due process and I think that would be a standard AFT position.

I don't want teachers who are in trouble to be left alone. I think that is what historically has been happening. Since I started teaching, we've learned a whole lot about how to help teachers. We've done enough research on teaching to know how to help a person become a better teacher.

Learning from Effective Teachers

There are behaviors that I think are important for schools. I got them from family, I got them from the union work, and I got them from colleagues in math. You begin to look at what happens in a much broader context, not just in the classroom.

Teaching is a craft. You watch craftsmen and you see how they learn their trade. They learn it from each other. I'd like to have some kind of a structure like that where you have some people who are novices, and then you have the journeymen, and you have the masters. All carpenters are working with wood, and all teachers should be working with kids. We're a long way from it, but I think there are more people who have this in their sights than ever before. When the education reform movement has more of those characteristics, I think it's going to be able to make some more progress.

In the last 20 years people have been going into classrooms and observing good teaching. Now, how do you know it's good teaching? You just ask everybody, then start looking at what effective teachers do. You begin to find commonalities among the effective teachers. Staff developers have found ways of communicating effective strategies. In EQUALS you do that. In our little county offices around the state we're talking about effective instructional techniques. We've begun talking about teachers helping teachers—coaching. We're beginning to talk to teachers about higher order thinking skills and effective questioning skills, about alternative approaches to discipline.

You know, 20 years ago this really didn't seem to be part of the body of knowledge. There was a lot of stuff about education, but there wasn't much about teaching. So we are now at the point where, if there's a teacher in my school who's having trouble, and if there's a skilled group of people who can observe and talk with the teacher, they can ask, "Well, what are the problems?" The teachers generally know what the problems are. They can begin to define strategies and sources of aid. I honestly believe that almost everyone who's having trouble can be given help to become better, or a good enough teacher to function. Maybe not great, but just become good enough. The few that don't, you've got to fire.

The Teacher in Public View

When I was teaching in Fond du Lac, Wisconsin, in the fall of 1963, there were about 35,000 people in the town and two schools: one public high school and a Lutheran high school. There were restrictions, and I was told certain things I couldn't do. I had to go with the dress code. I couldn't be seen smoking anywhere in the community, or go into a bar or a restaurant that served liquor anytime. This accounts for why I used to bump into all kinds of teachers in the bars in Ripon 20 miles away.

Men had a different salary schedule from women. Even if the woman was head of household, it was a low schedule. I remember when teachers were trying to get a pay increase, there was a letter to the editor of the local newspaper that said, "Why do these teachers need more money? They only work nine months a year. And with what they make working at the canneries in the summer, they do just fine." Everyone in my department there had an extra job, like working at Sears Friday night and Saturday.

Later on, when I was teaching in Glendale I got laid off because a tax override election failed, and they had to have a 15 percent cut. So they started by cutting 15 percent of the district office. You know, that sounds pretty good, but then those guys all had claims in the schools, so then they're cutting 15 percent of the administration and counseling, and it ended up with more than 15 percent of the teachers going.

State Purse Strings and the Leveling Process

As a funding source, the community is no longer relevant. California schools are funded on a state basis, not on a local basis. Beginning with SB 90 in 1972 and ending with Prop. 13 in 1978, with *Serrano* thrown in between, we've had a kind of leveling.[2] School districts that at one time were spending a lot more have essentially been leveled out, and districts that were underspending have moved up a lot. We've been under highly restricted growth policies, and in addition we've had a declining base, so our expenditures per pupil in this district are not more than other districts. In addition, we suffer from declining enrollments and, with income tied to attendance, we get less money each year.

Equity and Equality in Funding

It's probably true that our kids at Tam are getting better schooling than kids in Oakland, but it doesn't have to do with the current expenditures. They're probably spending more in Oakland. It doesn't cost as much to educate a kid at Tam as it does to educate a kid in Oakland. You have to provide whatever a person needs. This community doesn't really have enough to provide for its kids, but Oakland's kids need more. The only way you can have equal treatment is to give them more. Any time you treat everybody the same you're going to be unfair. That's what's happening in school funding. It's unfair to a lot of people.

In a democratic society you can't say that the quality of education is directly linked to the income of the community, to the wealth of the community. We could take care of the size of California's school classes by not producing a couple of these aircraft carriers, or some of the weapons systems. Our schools are used every day.

Education and the Class Structure

We're underfunded, not just in California, which is critically underfunded, but around the country. We're in another situation where our knowledge base is well beyond our ability to implement it. That's OK because that gives us targets. I don't think this society has ever placed a high priority on young people. I don't think this society has ever had a real commitment to mass education; for one thing, I think it's too dangerous.

It was important for social and political reasons to get kids in schools, but the schools were always a multi-layered system. The relatively recent phenomenon of all these people going on into further education is an out-of-control accident in many ways for the people who really run this society. A reaction is the big push for vocational education. What they're saying is, "We've got to divert some people out of higher education into these alternatives because we're going to have too many people going for control."

I see that on class lines. There aren't as many positions at the top, and there are more people whose children are eligible for those positions than ever before. So you take a look at the reactionary policies of the Reagan administration to essentially cut access to higher education for people who can't afford it on their own; that is perpetuating a class position. I don't think there's been a lot of fluidity among classes, but there has been a degree of it that's threatening.

Look at other things: childcare. How can this society with all its resources not provide childcare? You just look at what goes into resources for children. The attention that's focused on children is profit-making attention. It's in the marketplace, it's not here in the schools. How can you have a society as advanced as ours that doesn't guarantee at least that every child is going to have all the medical care it needs?

There's going to have to be a fundamental shift in society. The business community is dissatisfied with the neglect of schools and young people in California. It can't pursue its interests without a properly educated workforce. It can't sell its products. So we're seeing in California a new role in the business community advocating reform in education, reform in the schools, including funding.

Questions in Mid-Career

Well, thinking about my career is the hard part. I've been in kind of a state of flux. After about seven or eight years of teaching, I got a little bored with it. I don't mean to say that I was so good at it that I didn't have anything to learn, but the initial challenge was gone. I got more heavily involved with union work, because this was an area that was related to what I was doing, but I needed new knowledge. I've gotten pretty good at it. I'm vice-president of California Federation of Teachers, the state affiliate of AFT. I'm no longer very active in my local. I assist the local; that interest sustained me for a long time.

Then I got interested in the California Mathematics Project at [UC] Davis, and I have been excited about EQUALS.[3] The first day I showed up I knew that somewhere in place was really good staff development for teachers, and before that I hadn't been sure. We did a lot of good work around this school, got girls involved in math. For about three years I was going out and doing workshops and having a lot of fun on problem-solving stuff, and then I wasn't sure what I wanted to do.

As for the notion of career ladders, there aren't any: there's up and out. You either are in teaching or you are not. I don't like the notion of not teaching, and I don't like the notion of getting into one of those administrative positions the way it is now, because then I'll lose all my friends, or the few friends that I have, and lose the relationships that I have with teachers. Even being released from teaching, the way I am right now, there are a lot of people whose attitudes toward me have changed, people who have been friends for years. Misery likes miserable company, and while I'm working hard at my job, I'm not miserable. Many of my colleagues are working hard in their jobs and it's become miserable for them, and they don't have options, they just have work.

I have options at this place, right now. I like this new project [on dropout prevention], and I'm trying to figure out what I want to do next. My wife doesn't want me to go into administration. I don't really want to go into administration, but any administration that I had would be different. If it weren't different, I'd get out because my identity is as a teacher, not as an administrator. I get into trouble with the principal from time to time, but I'm completely secure because the worst thing that anybody can do to me is something that I truly like to do. I mean, they can give me the worst math kids around here, and I like to do that. So, I'm more free in that respect. I'm more my own boss.

I'm in the middle of a career trying to figure out what I want to do. I understand that it's one of the stages that one goes through. My superintendent sends me job notices daily now. "Principal, El Dorado High School." That's a good one for you. The last job notice I got had an envelope with it. He must have really liked that one. But I don't want to leave Tam High. There is a kind of security-consciousness that teachers have.

Part of my problem is that I'm not as interested in math education as I once was but I'm more interested in general kinds of education issues, and there are no places for that. You can become a principal or you teach.

Range of Salaries, Range of Roles

"Career ladders" is a mixed bag because in most people's minds it is a euphemism for merit pay. It's a way of saying, "Yes, come on into teaching. You can start at $20,000 and make as much as $75,000." But if only 2 percent of the teachers are making $75,000, it's a phony promise.

I do like the idea of a much wider range of salaries, and a much wider range of roles. Last year I was teaching five classes in the same building I had been in 20 years earlier. My role and responsibilities hadn't changed, and that's the way it is with all of my colleagues, whether we're beginners or mentors.

On a Teacher Exchange in England

Two years ago I had a Fulbright in England, a teacher exchange. I was in Bournemouth on the south coast. It was a wonderful experience for me. I was working in a girls' school, ages 11 to 16, younger than I'd ever worked with before. I just had a great time with the 1st, 2nd, and 3rd years, the youngest kids. It was one of these situations where the kids loved their teacher. They still do love their teacher.

I taught in my style, which is very different from the English style: no hollering, no humiliations. I did the same thing I do here. I went into these classes under the assumption that these girls could do whatever it was I wanted them to do. Maybe they had to stretch. The young ones just loved it. I remember doing problem-solving stuff; it was wonderful. They had some great materials that they had just adopted. The older girls were tougher, less flexible because they were in exam-oriented courses.

I didn't realize what kind of school I was in until a few months after I was there. It wasn't an academic school. The top 15 percent went to another school. These were the other kids who knew they were "fifth set" and they said, "You can't give us that, Mr. Gold. We're the fifth set." But still they could do it, and I didn't lower my expectations.

Pastoral Care, Responding to Students' Concerns

While it was not a strong academic school, it had a very strong pastoral care program. It's the student-service end of a school rather than the academic instruction services; they call it pastoral because these are schools from a religious tradition. You know, there is an official church in England. The only course that's required in England is Religious Education. Some of that stuff is really good, and some of it's terrible, but they pay a lot of attention to the kids. When one of these girls would come in and be upset about something, there's an adult to talk to—whether it's the form teacher, like the homeroom teacher, or their head of house—there's someone working for the kids.

I took a look at that aspect of working with kids, and I came back here and thought about kids in our community. So many of them are involved with substance abuse, so many are involved with dysfunctional families, with single parents who are working so hard to just keep the family together they haven't got enough time for the kids. When this job came along here, I didn't see it so much as drop-out prevention as providing support.

I made some proposals around the school along these lines. We need an expanded program of support services. Now, they're not well accepted, because it means a change in the role of the teacher. I do think that you have to respond to the kids, whether it's in the math class or the English class or somewhere else. Some of these kids are just not able to do math, day after day, but if we could respond to some of their other concerns I think we can get them doing it. We can help them in those areas and we can also get to the math deficit. I've got some ideas along those lines.

Disappearance of Alternative Learning Approaches

This year I'm coordinating a special project at Tam High and I only teach one class. I was chosen for my leadership ability, and because no one else applied. The project is in the category of dropout prevention. Part of the first wave of school reform, which increased requirements across the board, has also had the impact of increasing the dropout rate. At this school, we don't have a high dropout rate, compared to San Francisco or Oakland, San Jose, or L.A., but we have an increased number of kids at risk of not graduating.

Because there has been an increase in academic requirements and a decrease in funding, there has been a consequent elimination of programs and courses in which these kids, who are now at risk, had a lot more success. Our fine arts, and our technical arts in particular, are disappearing like crazy. We're sitting in a room that used to be an art metal room. A lot of creative kids who weren't that academically interested and connected, were successful in here. It's gone. We're down to two wood shop classes, no metal shop anymore. It wasn't so much that we had a lot of kids in there who weren't bright—we also had a lot of kids who were bright—but we had kids who learned in different ways. Those alternative learning approaches are disappearing and, in part, it's a direct consequence of underfunding and the first wave of reform.

There are outrageous numbers of people in this society who are being turned out as functional illiterates with diplomas. It's getting to the point where a lot of people see that the very fabric of this society is going to be torn. How can these people participate as citizens?

Kids Who Could be Doing Better

As Al Shanker of the AFT has said, "We're doing a little bit better for the 20 percent with whom we were succeeding in the first place." What about the others? We need to be doing different kinds of things in schools. The project I'm involved with focuses on 9th and 10th graders who are capable of doing better than they're doing. They're not special education kids, they're not handicapped kids. They may come from families that are dysfunctional. They may have just been in a syndrome of failure. They may have been involved in substance abuse problems. They may learn in different ways. They just don't do as well as they can. We got some funding to try a pilot, evolve a model that would be appropriate in this kind of community, because we don't qualify for funding for dropout prevention from the usual sources.

We've got between 60 and 70 kids. Mostly we've just been focusing on study skills and self-esteem. It's just one period a day, an elective class. I've been doing a lot of work to get people to realize that these aren't special education kids who are handicapped but they're kids who were maybe troublesome and, if they keep going at the rate they're going, they're not going to graduate. Anecdotally I know that we're successful. Teachers say the kids are doing a whole lot better. But it's a short program; how much can you change? We do let them come in for a second year. We're developing a model. Eighty percent of the positive stuff is that you're in there with a teacher who cares and gets the opportunity to demonstrate that.

I don't believe in this rugged individualism crap, and I think that a lot of the failure in school has been based on the transmission of that belief and the acting out of that belief. The research shows that when a teacher calls for an answer and kids raise their hands and teacher calls on a kid in less than one second, that's individualism. Calling on one kid to give the answer is ridiculous. There are other kinds of techniques that we know of. Just have the kids write something down. They can show it to a neighbor. Everybody gets a right answer, everybody gets recognition, but this is not part of some of our cultures.

Time, Conditions of Work, and the Professionalizing of Teachers

Teachers have a lot of power, but they're not going to be able to release this potential with the schools organized the way they are now. So there's a dilemma. I don't think it's an irresolvable one. Part of it is funding; that's related to time. American teachers are so busy that they just can't focus directly on their load of responsibility.

I was talking to a Japanese teacher last week who teaches the equivalent of 16 hours a week. The American teacher teaches 25 or 30 hours in the secondary school. In elementary school how many of these people are just locked in with kids and still don't have preparation time where they can sit down and do any professional thinking? There's no time for collegial work as part of our job. Those things are going to have to change.

One of the great incentives to change is that, if we don't make the profession attractive to people like me and the ones that came in when I did in the 60s—who are not in the bottom 25 percent but have all kinds of choices—then we're going to have empty classrooms. That is, empty of adults and full of kids. As I look at all the statistics, at least a third of all college graduates would have to go into teaching in California to maintain the same level we have right now, which is the highest class size in the country. We're not going to get a third of all college graduates. We can make inroads to increase that number we do get, and we can draw back in a lot of people who are trained but not teaching, by looking at the working conditions and the notion about professionalizing teaching.

People who will come into teaching, particularly if there are hurdles, are going to be the kind of people who won't stay in teaching if it's going to be crap. They will, with their options, make it clear that there are going to have to be these changes. I believe that we can work with people who are coming in. A lot of the new people that we are getting are not young people anyway, they're middle-aged people transferring from other careers.

Teachers as a Progressive Force

Teachers can be a progressive force, and they can be an organized force, even within the existing political structure. For the most part, teachers' politics are more progressive than not.

The political power base for teachers, if they can organize through their unions, is just enormous. Nearly every community has central labor bodies, which are community organizations of working people, and every community in which they are located has teachers. These are very important, politically active groups. The association has no connection with these central bodies, but in areas where the AFT is, we're on these central bodies.

We present and articulate issues around the young people. With social workers in these county offices, we talk about their issues. The bartenders and the construction people who might be there, or the laundry workers, get to hear and understand our positions. All the politicos come to us for support. Around this country there could be a progressive force in every community that comes out of the teachers through their unions. The teachers are present in every community anyway. Even without their unions, they can be a progressive force, working with kids. Our ability to influence kids is enormous, and it's a responsibility we take very seriously.

Teaching, a Terrific Job

I think the second wave of reform is important. The first wave wasn't really reform, it was just requirements, the kind of things we've seen here in California. Bill Honig has been a great exponent of increased requirements, more homework, longer school days, trying to work harder and do better while doing more of the same. That's not going to change much.

The second wave of reform has to do with empowering teachers and establishing the profession, the real professionalization of teaching. That's going to be the key, where we talk about giving decision-making power, policy-making power at the local school site and the community to teachers and parents to decide what's really needed for kids. Right now that's not done. There are a number of structures, of collegial models, that I think are going to come into place in the schools.

We're going to be preparing teachers in a different way. The entrance requirements for teaching have to be strengthened substantially. There should be a very heavy hurdle to clear before getting in, and the hurdle should include an academic component, an internship process, perhaps a residency process where people who want to become teachers are working in schools with mentors who are teachers in the schools. It should take a couple of years. There are probably exam-type hurdles, although not necessarily subject-matter or stupid ones.

It's got to be hard. It's difficult to become an architect or an attorney or a C.P.A. or a contractor. It's easier to become a teacher than any of those things. If you're going to make it tough to get in, then you're going to have to be able to draw people. If you draw people, intelligent people, they're going to have to have teaching and learning conditions that make sense, and they're going to have to have salaries that are commensurate. I believe that there are a lot of people out there who would be drawn to teaching, with even a moderate increase in salary, if we could get to these other things. I do believe that there are people out there who care about kids, and they want job satisfaction.

Teaching is a terrific job without the crap. If we could get our workloads down to the point where we could focus on kids, where we could have our schedules so that we could plan together about what seems to work, we could share with each other.

If we could get into each other's classrooms to help each other the way Joe Gutierrez and I did in the late 60s, then everything is going to get better around the school. We'll be doing more of what the kids need. We'll be better at it. We'll be nicer to everybody.

Pull Toward Cooperative Learning

Reforming the schools through empowering teachers is going to lead to an increase in the ability of teachers to change what is going on in the classroom. We will see more cooperative learning, for example, and, just as the research shows, kids are going to learn better that way. Cooperative learning is in so many ways "unAmerican." It's certainly unWestern, but it's the way people work. People don't work by themselves.

I think we really need to equip people to work in society by doing that. So I'm beginning to look at more of the processes and wondering if maybe that's another area that I'd like to study. Math becomes an excellent vehicle for dealing with these social issues, in part because of its status, because it provides opportunity for advancement particularly for girls and minorities. I remember hearing someone once say, "You know, one of the most important reasons for teaching algebra is so that when kids finish it, for the rest of their lives they can say, 'I studied algebra and I did all right.'" That's true. We can do that with math.

I learned a lot about cooperative learning through the union. You couldn't do the work alone, but there was individual accountability. Nobody had answers, and everybody had bits to contribute. Ultimately we were all responsible. Now, when you take a look at the role of the teacher almost all that is absent. I've been here in this school for 24 years now and every principal that I've ever had—and I love some of these guys, I like the woman that we have now, and I've fought with all of them—at some time each one has said, "As principal, I'm responsible for everything that goes on here in this school." As soon as someone says to me that I'm not responsible, they're not going to get the best work from me. When someone says, "You're responsible," then I'm going to work harder, and I think kids will do the same thing.

We don't try to teach mathematics now without an experiential base that comes earlier, but we're trying to get teachers to do cooperative learning without any instruction. That's what attracted me toward being a principal. I would organize a school that would be centered around teachers, not the kids. Because if we can get teachers to be responsible, get them to work in collegial, cooperative ways, then we could talk about what goes on in their classrooms. I believe that what's good for teachers is good for students. The more empowered teachers are, the more likely it is that they're going to be available to respond to what kids really need in their classrooms. But they need an experiential base just like the seven-year-old needs to work with manipulatives.

Teachers and Parents: The Same Focus

It's very important that the people who are centered on kids recognize themselves as allies and not opponents. We teachers get a lot of attack from parents; teachers often attack parents when, in fact, we are the two groups who share exactly the same focal point, the same focus of interest: the kid.

The school board doesn't share that, the school administration doesn't share that, the politicians in the community don't share it. It's mom and me who care about little Amy in class. I think we need a recognition of that, and a breaking down of the barrier. We need to bring parents and teachers closer together in the schools, not just for the parents to come in and have bake sales, put out newsletters, and donate scholarship money and paint. Teachers and parents need to get in there and talk about the educational policies in the community.

What Keeps a Teacher Going

Yesterday in my 24 years of teaching, I had a first. A student at this school who's graduating, invited me to her house Sunday afternoon. She had invited about 10 of us who had been her teachers, for dinner. She essentially had us over to feed us and to thank us. We were all sitting at the table, and this 18-year-old kid went around the table and said to each one, "This is what you did for me." God. It was...[silent, very choked up] I get too emotional. Her mother said, "This is a teacher's dream. I was a teacher." There are other things that happen along the way. That's the first time it's happened that way.

I was in the locker room, taking a shower, and a guy across the room is taking a shower. I haven't got my glasses on. The kid's 28 or 30, and he says, "Didn't you used to be Mr. Gold? Didn't you used to work at Tam High?" I said, "Well, I'm still Mr. Gold and I still work there." I can't tell who he is. He tells me who he is, and he says, "I used to give you so much trouble," and I didn't remember much. Then he starts telling me about himself—he's a businessman now—and we walk out. I jump into my '64 Chevrolet and he jumps into his BMW.

He says, "You were really good, and you didn't let me get away with anything." I don't even remember him, but that's one of the things kids want. They don't want you to let them get away with it; if you let them get away with it, then you don't care. It always boils down to the care.

Notes

[1] The U.S. Supreme Court ruling threw out the "separate but equal" doctrine established in *Plessy v. Ferguson*, thus opening the door for eliminating segregation in public education.

[2] Senate Bill 90 (SB 90) 1972 was enacted into law by the California Legislature. The measure established a ceiling on the amount of money collected per pupil, based primarily on each district's revenue per pupil in 1972–73. This ceiling was known as the revenue limit. *Serrano v. Priest* was the 1976 California Supreme Court decision that declared California's system of financing schools unconstitutional because it violated the equal protection clause of the state Constitution. The court requires that: 1) differences in annual per pupil expenditures due to local wealth must not exceed $100, 2) the relative effort required of local taxpayers for school services must be nearly the same throughout the state, and 3) both pupils and taxpayers must receive equal protection under the law. Calif. Dept. of Education, *California Schools beyond Serrano: a report on Assembly Bill 65 of 1977* (Sacramento, CA 1978).

[3] The California Mathematics Project is a statewide mathematics inservice program. Contact Phil Daro, Office of the President, University of California, Kaiser Building, 300 Lakeside Drive, Oakland, CA 94612.

AFTERWORD: IDEAS IN PROGRESS

Our Afterword takes its starting point from the seven teachers who have shown us life in their classrooms: what they accomplish, what they hope for, what they and their students need, and what help we can provide. Children in every classroom need good teachers like those in this book.

These teachers invite us to understand how they try to connect with the feelings and abilities of every child, every day, in every class. These connections mean that each day's teaching requires a full measure of art, content, and creativity. However, the teaching conditions in many schools work against teachers' best efforts and discourage new entrants to the profession.

Let's imagine a time when the conditions have changed enough so that teaching is a highly valued profession. In that future, teachers will find emotional satisfaction, intellectual stimulation, and monetary rewards. What would it take to make this reversal occur: to transform teaching into a profession that you would encourage a promising student to choose? What would it take to involve you as an advocate for teachers?

We suggest that transforming the teaching profession into one with greater power to attract new teachers and retain experienced ones requires key changes, including:

1) development of public understanding and appreciation of what the teaching profession can accomplish at its best,

2) increased involvement of informed citizens on behalf of public schools, and

3) expanded resources so that teachers can provide students with the best possible learning experiences.

The teachers' concerns have led us to propose changes needed within the schools, including two new roles—the community linking teacher and the stystems worker. The community linking teacher can help build the schools' constituency, and the systems worker can directly address the out-of-school needs of the child. In addition, we recognize the importance of using time as an instrument of change by providing more adults in the classroom and more time for both students' and teachers' learning.

These changes offer new possibilities for what teachers can do and what students can learn, but a danger persists: The proposed changes cannot simply be grafted onto the present system, but must be seen as supportive of and depending on the emergence of a newer, more equitable educational system.

Building a Constituency for Schools

As each school day begins, many teachers close their classroom doors and define their own domains. They shut themselves in with their students, and for a time shut out the part of the community that can be hazardous and even destructive to children. School may be the only stable, safe place some children can find.

Teachers know, however, that the door cannot stay closed. As Sallyann Tomlin observed, teachers perceive the public as "not understanding what they [teachers] are all about." Teachers must welcome, or at least avoid alienating, those whose good will, support, and long-term commitment are crucial for sustaining both students and teachers—voters and decisionmakers, business and professional people, parents, the media, administrators, and politicians—individually, in small groups, and in sizable organizations. Teachers need both their trust and support.

It follows that teachers must expand their basic constituency beyond the classroom. Children cannot vote, and many of their distracted or disenchanted parents inadvertently punish the schools by failing to vote on major school funding issues. Even with good will, people may neglect to support good teachers and schools because, as potential voters, these citizens are detached or alienated from both the schools and the political process.

Some of the tradeoffs of political life can serve the schools, if teachers can identify and secure their benefits. Like other citizens, many teachers are aware of the political arena, but do not rush to take their places there. For some, political savvy and participation develop naturally. For others, the intense life of the classroom draws all their energies; they pour out their gifts of planning, questioning, listening, helping, and learning into work with their students, who are their first priority.

One who suggests that the excellent teachers in the second group should also serve as front-line public advocates for school support and funding must proceed with caution. Many teachers are now so overloaded with demands and requirements unaccompanied by funds or other support, that anything smacking of one more claim on their energies seems unrealistic.

Not all teachers, however, need to work in the public arena in the same way. Some thrive on political activism, on union work, on public outreach. They have the presence to address meetings, to testify in public hearings, to deal effectively with the media. Others, who see themselves exclusively as classroom teachers, may do their most constructive politicking as teachers— of individual parents, of decision-makers, of community organizations. They may be at their best one-to-one, face-to-face, talking with a potential school volunteer or with a legislator's aide, providing information to influence policy decisions.

In this country, public education is an integral part of the political process. The informed participation of the public, teachers, and legislators is essential for high-quality public education. This interdependence can be denied or ignored only at the peril of those who are most vulnerable—the children in school.

The bond that connects the teacher in the classroom to the voter in the polling booth may at times be burdensome, but it is necessary for good public education. To strengthen that bond will require a new effort to develop public understanding of the teaching profession.

For teachers to gain public respect and support, they must communicate with the public what they are doing and why. It is not enough for teachers to do their best job within the walls of their classrooms, because the larger public, including legislators, must understand more of what goes on in schools. We propose the community linking teacher to foster this public understanding.

Community Linking Teacher

Teachers are the most credible interpreters of school life. They have day-to-day experience of what is, and the vision of what could be. They can serve as interpreters to the world outside the classroom, but such a role cannot be imposed on every teacher. Instead we can create a new position, the community linking teacher, to close the gap between the classroom and the community.

The community linking teacher would develop a process of advocacy on behalf of the school by making it better known and understood throughout the community. Teachers in this role would inform the community and answer questions fully and with candor. They may find themselves at times embattled, sometimes welcomed, and often misunderstood. How do they learn to cope with public disinterest and cultivate support?

As in teaching, there is no one formula for success. Some community linking teachers will talk with local newspaper editors; others will wangle invitations to address community service clubs; still others may seek help in polishing their communication skills. There is no "teacher-proof" method of preparing for this role. Each community linking teacher needs the freedom to make connections in the way that is most personally comfortable.

We see this role as distinct from that of the principal, who in some communities does function effectively as a spokesperson for the schools, especially in those rare instances when the principal also teaches. However, it is the teacher in the classroom who can best communicate to the public the experience of the profession.

The Work of Linkage

Teachers in this role would develop leadership skills and contacts, benefitting both the schools and the public by increasing understanding on both sides. They would build a network of informed citizens and increase the base of advocates for the school. The cost would be the teachers' time away from teaching; the benefits include the school's losing its aura of alienation, recruiting a committed citizenry, and becoming an integral part of the community.

Since many good teachers would not choose to be out of the classroom full-time, the job could be part-time for at least two years. It could then be rotated to keep the "teacherliness" of the outreach and prevent it from becoming routine public relations. Each community linking teacher needs to convey to the next what has been learned, to build up a body of knowledge of what is needed and what works in that community.

The community linking teacher would not function in isolation but would gather a small committee of consultants. These could include the principal, one or two other teachers, and a few community people willing to work for constructive change. The committee, with rotating membership, could help the community linking teacher solve problems and provide an ongoing source of support. In smaller districts, one teacher might represent several schools, but under no conditions should this job be a part of the district-office administration. It is essential that the work of linkage reflect the classroom teacher's immediate experience, knowledge, and personality.

Helping Parents to Connect

Parents are key members of the schools' constituency, but often those who are most active in schools do not reflect the full diversity of the schools' population. Many parents do not see themselves as participating in school affairs or taking political action. Their detachment may have many sources: lack of time and energy for the single-parent head of family, haunting money worries, language barriers, or conviction that schools have their job, parents have theirs, and no mingling makes sense.

Even these detached parents can respond to invitation and enter into a mutually beneficial relationship with the schools. For example, the community linking teacher could connect with families by informing them of the FAMILY MATH program, in which parents and children learn mathematics together in a non-threatening and enjoyable way.[1] Through the program, parents gain insights into their own and their children's learning styles and experience the pleasure and pride of learning together with their children. FAMILY MATH provides a way for parents who are struggling in society to act on their profound commitment to their children's welfare. The experience of FAMILY MATH gives participating parents a clearer view of the mathematics their children need, and ways to obtain it for them. Having learned this much, parents often win enough confidence to guide the child's progress through school. For many parents, this is a new role.

Out-of-Class Support: The Systems Worker

Today's children bring to our schools two needs: to learn and to survive a society in turmoil. Suzy Ronfeldt alludes to the difficult, even desperate, condition of some of the children in her class. She and other teachers are drawn into issues of health care, safety, and legality that they often feel reluctant to handle.

Formerly in this country, school nurses, counselors, or school social workers responded to the out-of-class problems that children presented. Today, in many schools these positions no longer exist, but the children's problems remain, and the burden of responding to them falls largely on classroom teachers.

The situation is not quite the same in an English school where Frank Gold taught as a Fulbright Scholar. He noted that when students came to school upset about personal problems, there was an adult to help them with their concerns. He recognized two separate realms of school responsibility: student service and academic instruction. He was impressed by the effectiveness of the student-service function, in which each child could find a trained person who provided help with a wide range of problems.

Here at home, we can no longer expect teachers or principals to deal with the increasing numbers and severity of the children's problems. These problems require the attention of an adult who focuses entirely on the physical and emotional well-being of the child: a systems worker. This person should be able to understand and work through all available service systems: social welfare, health, and legal, to make appropriate choices and obtain the best help in each case. The urgent needs this country's children bring with them to school must not be allowed to overwhelm them. The role of a systems worker must be reinstated.

The teacher who can call on a systems worker for help can then concentrate on working with all the children in the class and devote precious time to what he or she does best—teaching.

Rethinking Schooling

The community linking teacher and the systems worker do not mask the need for more far-reaching reforms, since these roles will accomplish little if they give the illusion of reform without the substance. It is a hopeful sign that a number of the nation's school systems are working to provide reform with substance.[2] We must wait before we can fairly judge the outcomes of these experiments, and until more schools undergo the scrutiny and analysis that rethinking and restructuring requires.

The notion of rebuilding public education, of dealing with the problems of the present so that we also serve the future, requires us to question the "givens" of the past. Each school and community must undertake this rethinking to bring about both present improvement and long-term benefits.

Albert Shanker, President of the AFT, has observed that "The education profession will have to be restructured if schools are to make more intelligent use of their human resources...[Restructuring] is not simply a matter of developing career ladders, or involving teachers in decision making, or getting more computers....It requires rethinking all our assumptions about schools, from the eggcrate organization to the concept of class size, from age-grading to the uses of teachers' time."[3]

The roles of the community linking teacher and the systems worker are designed to ease the transition between present systems and their future forms, and can facilitate the process of evolution. Under newer and improved school conditions the need for these positions may in time disappear, and new functions will supersede them.

The Limits of a Teacher's Art

A good teacher can find many ways in the classroom to help each child to be successful. But as currently organized, the public school system does not support experiments, risk-taking, or much if any deviation from the norm. Teachers who buck the system risk hostility and repression at worst, or indifference at best, and it takes a toll on them. For major effective change to occur, a teacher's goals must mesh with those of the school faculty and administration, who must obtain support for such change from the district hierarchy and the school board.

The process of change can be erratic, and requires advocates with stamina and conviction. Change may begin when the school's faculty and the principal agree on the directions they want to pursue. This accord may take years to develop, while shifts in personnel and policies may subvert or cause the whole process to end. On the other hand, advocates may choose to move ahead with a few people who are sympathetic, and then wait for others either to follow, or to leave. In either case, lasting change involves a long-term process, and the kind of endless monitoring and evaluation that runs counter to the desire to get things settled once and for all.

The seven teachers in this book have had successes and achieved improvements in part because they have found or created hospitable school environments, but not every teacher can be so extraordinary or so lucky. Teachers can devise reforms classroom by classroom, but accomplish little in the long run unless reforms can spread beyond those bounds.

Along with advocates, the process of creating reform requires funds. When more adults are at work in the schools, funds must be provided to pay for every additional hour. As a political truism, schools receive more money when the electorate is willing to pay. Willingness to pay requires conviction that the money spent will bring solid benefits.

Present Costs, Future Benefits

While many adults love and prize their own and other children, American society overall appears not to value children as a group, nor does it care to give consistent attention to their well-being. One needs only to look at the inadequacy of provision for child care and the paucity of medical care for many, to see that children rank low among the public's funding priorities. Funding is a expression of support, and publicly voted funding for K–12 education demonstrates how close to the bone ballot measures can cut.

For example, two statewide ballot measures have influenced, if not skewed, the funding patterns of public education in California. Voters approved Proposition 13 in 1978, an initiative measure that cut locally levied property taxes and limited the taxing levels of local agencies. In 1984, they endorsed a state lottery that some saw as an alternative to taxation. These measures' intended and unintended consequences have deepened the teachers' unease over repeated threats of layoffs, unwieldy class size, and a feeling that the public's willingness to support taxes for public education may be slipping away.

Funds for the Community Linking Teacher and the Systems Worker

This erratic funding course suggests the need for a long-range response to overcome the unpredictability of school financing. Soft money in the form of grants can support new ventures in schools for a limited time. Such grants were once considered seed money to permit the demonstration of good ideas, with the hope that once such programs began, they would find a place in school budgets. In the 1990s however, public budgets have become so constrained that even prior commitments are suffering cuts, and seed money has lost its promise.

Furthermore, grantors from the private sector often hesitate to supplant what they see as the responsibilities of the public sector. In addition, some may be reluctant to commit support, indefinitely or even for the long term, to a limited set of programs. Thus soft money now signals instability, and the demise of programs that depend upon it.

The role of soft money in support of promising experiments, however, remains a valuable one. This role should be recognized as filling a particular niche—encouraging innovation—and not be confused with the funding philosophy of long-term investments in essential programs that require continuity and stability to accomplish their goals.

If soft money is unsatisfactory, hard money—tax or publicly committed funds with all its political uncertainties—remains the basic alternative for the long run. Tax funds can shift from year to year, but continue to be more nearly dependable as a source for ongoing support of public schools, if public support can be sustained.

Some taxpayers have ruefully likened appeals for school funds to the antics of a family member who writes home only to ask for money. There is a kind of truth in these complaints, that citizens hear about schools primarily when money is needed, either through a tax increase or a bond issue. One cannot entirely fault the schools for this state of affairs, since normal school activities seldom pre-empt the nightly news. The usual public relations of schools can hardly compare with the more colorful efforts of others who compete for public attention, or the fearsome demands of war.

For this reason, we advocate the position of the community linking teacher as a first priority. This is the best way we can see of establishing a compelling and immediate case for public support of the schools, and laying the groundwork for better times in the future.

We suggest that the role of the community linking teacher is so crucial that this position be established immediately with current resources. Schools always have found ways to reallocate existing resources, however small, when change was deemed essential. The community linking teacher represents the hope for a new relationship between schools and the public.

The next priority is the role of the systems worker who demonstrates commitment to the child's welfare and frees the teacher to concentrate on the challenges of teaching.

Schools are in a vulnerable position now but they are also poised for change. Recognizing what teachers and students need at this time is the first step in making improvements come about. Planning comes first, with discussion, decision, and implementation to follow.

If we do not start with planning now, opportunities may slip away if funds become more plentiful. We need to do what we can when money is scarce or virtually unavailable, and to know exactly what we want to do when funds are at hand. Tax money remains the basic, ongoing potential source of support for public education.

Today's Reality and the Teachers' Response

Public schools show us the varied faces of today and forecast those of tomorrow. As demographics change, children in our nation's public schools present an ever-widening range of diversity in race, culture, ethnicity, language, income levels, and physical capacities. Such diversity is not new in American society, but its range and magnitude have expanded. We are a country undergoing transformation; a new nation is emerging, one that is neither largely White nor middle class.

Most schools are not prepared for this transformation. The evidence of failure appears in unacceptable dropout rates in high schools and in elementary schools as well; and in the prevalence of tracking as a sorting device to deal with early failures in the process of teaching and learning. Tracking often relegates children of low income and of color to lower tracks and lower expectations. Both the drop-out rates and the consequences of tracking have signalled a painful reality. Our present system of public education is not serving well the majority of students now of school age nor will it serve those knocking at the door.

Disadvantage and Blame

Some observers offer constructive interpretations for dealing with present reality. Luis C. Moll notes that "There is nothing about minority children's language, culture or intellect that should handicap their schooling...These children are disadvantaged only to the extent that their parents and communities lack political power." He says that being disadvantaged "is not a characteristic or trait of the children, it is something done to the children."[4]

Leslie A. Hart urges school people to give up the comfortable habit of blaming the victim. He sees that the "vast majority continue to blame society, the community, the students' homes, television, drugs, lean school budgets, or whatever, as though the real problem were that too many parents are sending the wrong kind of children to school...

"[T]eachers, administrators, and policy makers at every level must focus on serving the students who come, doing to the fullest whatever the schools' resources permit—which can be very different from what the schools do with their resources today."[5]

The Teachers Find Alternatives

The seven exemplary teachers in this book do not indulge in blame, but look for opportunities. They invite us to see classroom life and recognize the reality of today's public school systems. They ask us to appreciate how diverse their students are, and to acknowledge the lack of fit between today's students and traditional public school organization.

As we have seen, the seven teachers reject traditional ways of teaching, traditions that seat children in rows, give them worksheets from outdated textbooks, and tell them to memorize rules or events that have no meaning for the students. Instead these teachers find alternative methods that involve children in grappling with interesting questions, thinking creatively, and revealing the excitement of learning to solve problems in their own ways. Teachers who embrace alternatives know that nothing can work all the time with all students, and that every child, every day, presents a new situation to be understood. To do this work, teachers need time.

Turning Time to Teachers' Advantage

The teachers' most urgent concern is the need for more time, and the element of limited time runs through many aspects of teaching. Time limits affect teachers' ability to plan for individuals and groups and to cultivate in each child the way he or she learns best. Those limits also affect teachers' opportunities to experiment and learn from success and failure, and to work with colleagues in teaching and revising the school's curriculum. Teachers need the greatest possible control over the ways they use available time.

In-Class Support for Teachers

The ratio of students to teacher curbs any teacher's effectiveness, because time limits determine how often a teacher can connect with children, individually or in groups. In California, a typical elementary school classroom houses 30 children and one teacher, who are often closeted together for six hours a day. It is virtually impossible for one teacher to foster each child's growth and keep close track of 30 children daily. Some teachers function better with larger numbers than others do, but every one experiences a limit, within narrow margins, beyond which teaching and learning suffer. Suzy Ronfeldt observes that with a 30 to 1 ratio, interactive teaching becomes an overwhelming task. Very few teachers can work well alone with more than 25 students at once, and none would wish to.

Even with smaller class sizes, each teacher will likely have at least one student, and often more, who need long-term, individual attention. In the past, these students were often pulled out of class to work with another adult. We know now, however, that "pull-out" programs are often unsuccessful because they stigmatize the child, emphasize rote learning, provide a curriculum that is inferior to that of the other students, and deprive the child of learning from and with classmates. The more humane and promising solution is to provide more high-quality, long-term adult assistance in the classroom.

We know teachers need more help in the classroom, but not all kinds of help are equally useful to all teachers. For many teachers, another peer in the classroom would be ideal. Student teachers, volunteers, and aides can provide another pair of hands, but at times this value can be offset by their demands on the teacher's time. The teacher must decide whether the time spent in teaching helpers is worth the time lost in teaching their students.

Elois Irvin finds the time with student teachers to be well spent. She noted that working with a student teacher made her more reflective of her own teaching. As she said, "If I didn't encounter a student teacher every now and then, I think I would forget how really hard it is to get things in place."

Grace Coates' experience as an aide motivated her to become a teacher, but her response is not typical. She found her training as an aide both disappointing and boring; it was "all the 'how to do' physical labor parts of being a teacher and none of the 'how to help the child'..."

Creating a professional path for aides would open the door for community people who might not otherwise consider higher education. The benefit of a professional view of aides would include a broadened source of potential teachers and a closer linking of the schools to the community.

Bob Whitlow sees the value of having parents actively teaching in his program, no matter how difficult that is. "It pays off. These parents get to see how hard my job is. The parents are interacting with the kids, they're learning a lot about each other, and the whole family unit is richer for it."

Whether the extra pair of hands belongs to a parent or an aide, in-class support for teachers benefits everyone. The teacher gains insight from the other adult as well as more time for students; the long-term adult assistant finds reward as well as new career options.

Time for Teachers' Learning

All of the seven teachers have expressed the importance of working collegially to continue their learning, and the difficulties of doing so in the regular school day. Teachers search eagerly for new ideas and content to bring to their students. Where curriculum specialists have been eliminated through budget cuts, teachers are thrown back on their own resources, and their consultation time with each other becomes even more important. Good teachers are not willing to pass on an impoverished curriculum to their students. They insist on curriculum improvement and require adequate time to make that possible.

Sallyann Tomlin describes ways in which teachers can be released to work with other colleagues or to attend professional development programs; these include minimum days or having principals take over classes. These arrangements are extremely rare in most public schools. Only Nan Jackson says that at her school, "...we are expected to take courses and workshops, or attend conferences, and we have the time and financial support to do that." She teaches at a private high school.

The opportunity to develop and expand one's expertise is an essential attribute of a desirable profession and a necessary condition for teachers' continual professional growth.

More Time for Students' Learning

The tyranny of time in the school day and year produces a number of problems for teachers and students, including artificial limits that create barriers to learning. Often, school time is broken into 45- to 55-minute periods and trimmed to fit shortened school days, semesters, and years. In middle schools and high schools, the scheduling of class periods prevents teachers from allowing students to pursue a topic or an idea over a period of weeks, an opportunity that could lead them to new learning. Frank Gold describes the importance of extending the traditional class period when he was creating an innovative math program.

In addition, teachers must spend time at year's end preparing their students for the transition to next year's teacher. As the next year begins, teachers must again take time to get acquainted with a new group of students. Students also lose learning time when they must readjust to teacher changes year after year in every class. One response to this time drain is to have children remain in "family" groups with the same teachers for a period of years, as Bob Whitlow does.

More time for learning could be gained by removing artificial limits such as class periods, or school semesters, or even the school year. Some schools have experimented with lengthening school time; more such experimentation would be useful. Expanding schedules and lengthening class time would require more teacher time in the classroom, and added hours must be paid for. Creative juggling can help, but increased funds will be needed.

Voices That Stimulate Change

Each of these teachers' voices differs from the others, as much as their experiences and lives do, but they are similar in significant ways. All are daring; all question the present system. The possibility of finding something better keeps them searching.

At times, their individuality places them at different points on important issues. Their disagreements give evidence of what they teach. First, there is more than one way to solve problems; and second, the bigger the problems, the more thoughtful people are needed to solve them. This is why each of us is needed to join in the informed constituency of public education.

The teachers' wisdom should challenge us to pay attention to public education and determine our most effective role in supporting schools. None of the advocated improvements will take place unless more of us make public education a personal priority. There are at least two ways to do this. They are both important, and individual preference will dictate which comes first. One is to support school funding issues and political candidates who work on behalf of the schools. Another is to become involved in a more personal way in local schools. Both can lead to sustained action that supports the best in public education, and responds directly to the aspirations of good teachers.

Good teachers are national assets. What they know and do is of lasting value, and their gifts are too precious to be wasted. When national assets speak, it is useful to listen. The rest of us who do not share their experiences can share their insights.

These teachers have earned the right to ask for our best efforts: willingness to listen and learn; generosity to match their own; stamina to last at least a few generations; and the daring to be visionaries both now and in the future.

Notes

[1] For more information, write to Virginia Thompson, Director FAMILY MATH, Lawrence Hall of Science, University of California, Berkeley, CA 94720.

[2] See, e.g., Carl D. Glickman, "Pushing School Reform to a New Edge: The Seven Ironies of School Empowerment," *Phi Delta Kappan*, September 1990, 68–75. See also Jane L. David, et al., *Restructuring in Progress: Lessons from Pioneering Districts* (Washington, D.C.: National Governors' Association, 1989).

[3] Shanker, "A Proposal for Using Incentives to Restructure Our Public Schools," *Phi Delta Kappan*, January 1990, 348.

[4] Moll, "Social and Instructional Issues in Educating 'Disadvantaged' Students," in M.S. Knapp, and P.M. Shields, eds., *Better Schooling for the Children of Poverty: Alternatives to Conventional Wisdom—Volume II Commissioned Papers and Literature Review* (Menlo Park, CA: SRI International, 1990) p. III-1.

[5] Hart, "The Horse is Dead," *Phi Delta Kappan*, November 1989, 239. For another thoughtful discussion of the ways children are disadvantaged by current educational practices, see Ralph Parish, et al., "Knock on Any School," *Phi Delta Kappan*, January 1989, 386-394.

WRITERS' NOTES

Nancy Kreinberg

The stimulus for this book occurred when I overheard Suzy Ronfeldt, a teacher I knew only by reputation, discussing how she felt about receiving a layoff notice from her district. I was stunned that this could occur and unaware that teachers of her stature were being treated in this way. Even though I had been working in the education profession for many years, there was much I had to learn.

My experience as an education writer and editor had not given me the kind of inside knowledge of the profession that my EQUALS colleagues had who had been classroom teachers. Working with them to create and conduct EQUALS over the years, I developed great admiration for their knowledge of the craft and sensitivity to the demands upon teachers from within and outside the school system. Together we created a program that expressed respect for teachers' experience, and acknowledged the time and effort required to change established practices.

The teachers who participated in EQUALS workshops often stated their exhilaration at having the opportunity to talk with other teachers about difficult issues and their appreciation for being treated as colleagues and peers. Their gratitude for such small tokens of respect aroused my concern. These were people with undeniable talent and skills, good teachers, trying to become better. Many were great teachers, and none of them had received the recognition nor the support they deserved and needed to do their job.

I wanted to write a book that would honor teachers and enable others to gain more understanding and appreciation for them. I knew the book should be in their voices and from their perspectives. Once I had conducted the interviews with the teachers, I wanted to work with someone who could respect the material and give it form and structure. I had known Harriet Nathan professionally for many years and felt very fortunate when she agreed to be a co-author of this book. The learning process continued for me as, out of our personal, professional, and political experiences, we shaped the book together.

In the end, the book became my way to advocate for teachers, and to repay them for teaching me about caring, commitment, integrity, and their profession.

Harriet Nathan

About ten years ago Nancy Kreinberg wrote two papers for the *Public Affairs Report* (PAR) series published by the Institute of Governmental Studies at UC Berkeley. They were titled "Math Avoidance for Women," and "1000 Teachers Later," both discussions of the EQUALS program. As principal editor at the Institute and co-editor of the PAR, I recognized the significance of these papers and the information they provided. That response was matched by those of thousands of readers who requested copies.

It was clear that the EQUALS program carried hope and promise, and that both math and public schools were far more interesting than I had imagined, even though my family and I had attended public schools and four immediate family members were fine teachers. My primary interests focused on the structure and function of government and the role of the informed citizen. Working in the League of Women Voters before returning to UC for a second degree in journalism served to sharpen an interest in these areas. Consequently, thinking about teachers and public schools also meant thinking about the political and governmental realities in which they function.

When Nancy invited me to join in working on this book of interviews, she had already spoken of the excellent teachers in the EQUALS program and the importance of what they knew and could do. The notion of interviews was most appealing, partly as a result of my work in the Regional Oral History Office of The Bancroft Library, where tape-recorded and transcribed interviews preserved the actual words of the narrators. Also, in the book *Critical Choices in Interviews: Conduct, Use, and Research Role* (U. C. Berkeley: IGS, 1986), I paid my respects to the power of interviews and the issues that surround them.

The seven good teachers who gave these interviews revealed their thinking with such immediacy and wisdom, that although I have read their words many times, I will continue to read them again and again.

INDEX